APPALACHIAN
SPRING

APPALACHIAN SPRING

Eleanor Gustafson

ZONDERVAN BOOKS
of ZONDERVAN PUBLISHING HOUSE
GRAND RAPIDS, MICHIGAN

THIS IS A ZONDERVAN BOOK
PUBLISHED BY ZONDERVAN PUBLISHING HOUSE
1415 Lake Drive, S.E.
Grand Rapids, Michigan 49506

Appalachian Spring
Copyright © 1984 by Eleanor Gustafson

Library of Congress Cataloging in Publication Data

Gustafson, Eleanor.
Appalachian spring.

I. Title.
PS3557.U835A86   1984   813'.54   84-2346
ISBN 0-310-37381-6

Book Designer: Martha Bentley
Copy Editor: John Iwema
Editor: Judith E. Markham

Printed in the United States of America

84 85 86 87 88 89 / 10 9 8 7 6 5 4 3 2 1

The harsh moon shines
On the iron river.
I shall not go down to the bank tonight
For all the dark shapes
And terrible phantoms
Cluster with a vengeance
Outside the door.
Oh it is long and long
I have guarded the treasure
Across my knees the hard sword drawn.

— D. Rice

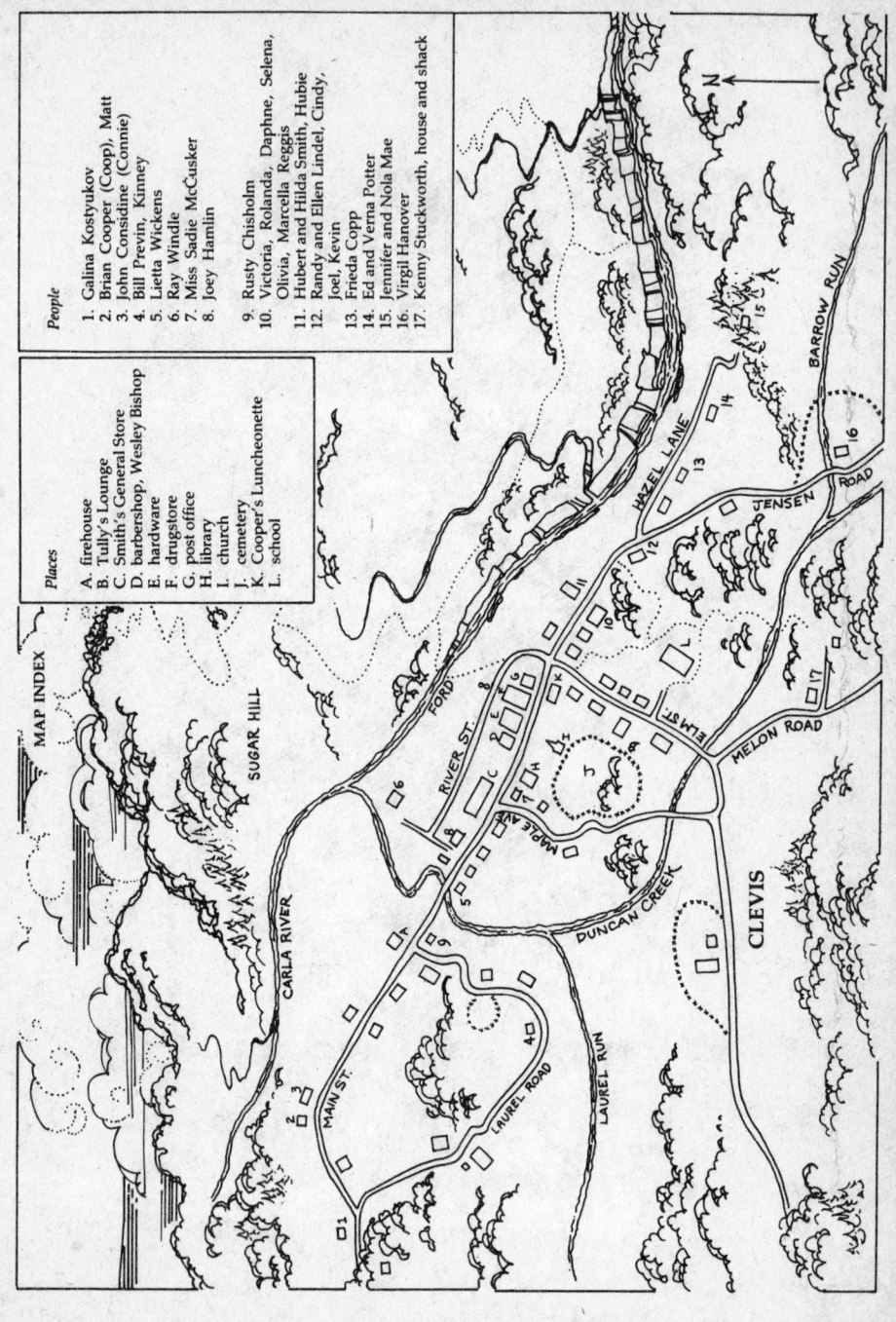

MAP INDEX

Places

A. firehouse
B. Tully's Lounge
C. Smith's General Store
D. barbershop, Wesley Bishop
E. hardware
F. drugstore
G. post office
H. library
I. church
J. cemetery
K. Cooper's Luncheonette
L. school

People

1. Galina Kostyukov
2. Brian Cooper (Coop), Matt
3. John Considine (Connie)
4. Bill Previn, Kinney
5. Lietta Wickens
6. Ray Windle
7. Miss Sadie McCusker
8. Joey Hamlin
9. Rusty Chisholm
10. Victoria, Rolanda, Daphne, Selena,
    Olivia, Marcella Reggis
11. Hubert and Hilda Smith, Hubie
12. Randy and Ellen Lindel, Cindy,
    Joel, Kevin
13. Frieda Copp
14. Ed and Verna Potter
15. Jennifer and Nola Mae
16. Virgil Hanover
17. Kenny Stuckworth, house and shack

SUGAR HILL

CARLA RIVER

MAIN ST.

LAUREL ROAD

LAUREL RUN

DUNCAN CREEK

MAPLE AVE

RIVER ST.

FORD

HAZEL LANE

JENSEN ROAD

BARROW RUN

ELM ST.

MELON ROAD

CLEVIS

N

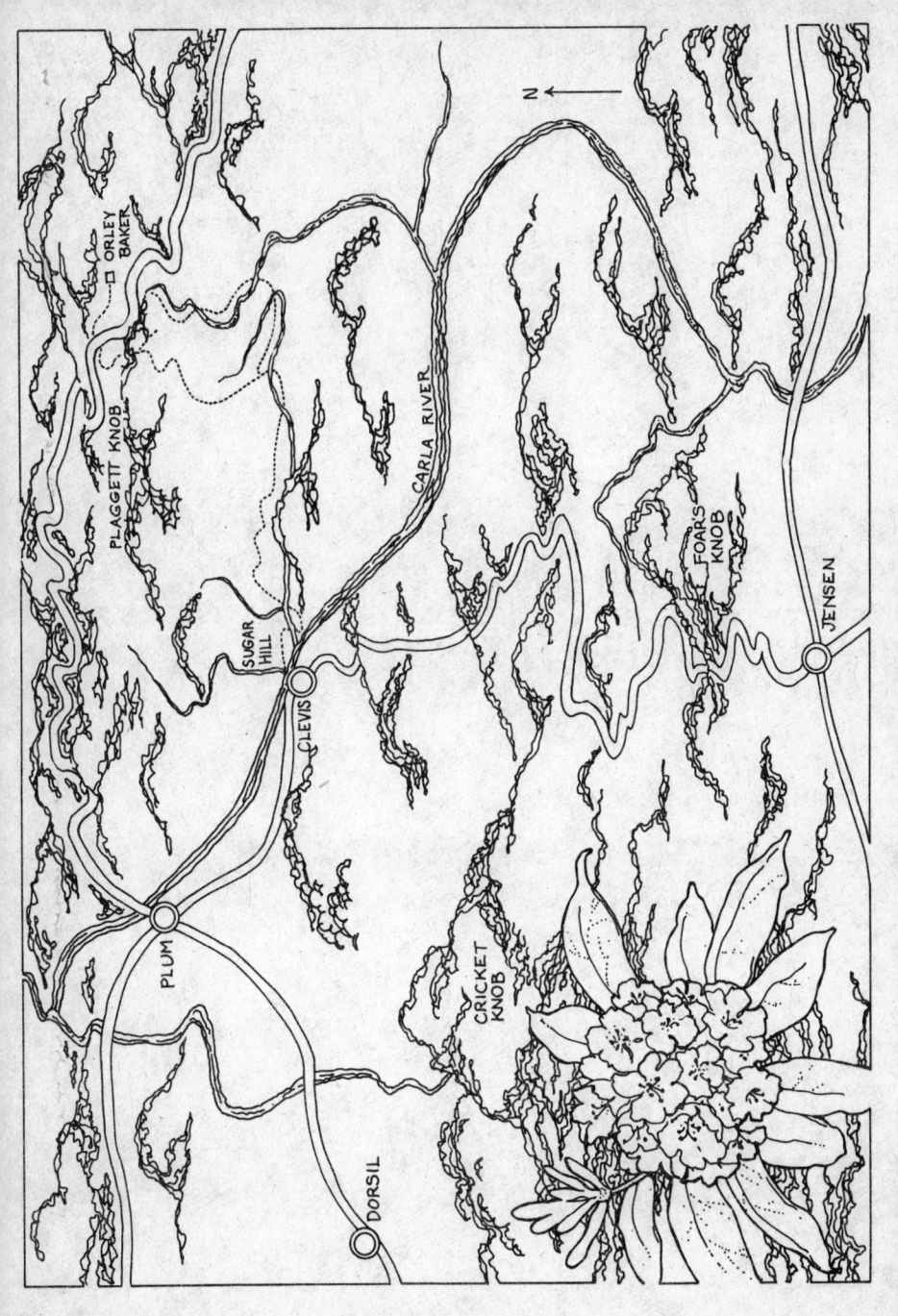

1

Jennifer had never heard *Appalachian Spring* before living with Nola Mae. Her first impression, that it was just another long, boring record, changed near the end when she recognized a melody that spun out and danced around in fugal fashion.

"That's a Christian song!" she said in surprise.

Nola Mae gave her a withering look. "It's an old Shaker tune called 'Simple Gifts.' "

They listened in silence until the last few notes melted away. "It *does* sound a lot like spring," Jennifer commented.

Nola Mae carefully lifted the record from the turntable and slipped it back into its jacket. "I heard Aaron Copland himself say that he didn't have spring in mind at all when he composed it. He wrote it as ballet music for Martha Graham, but I don't suppose you'd know anything about her. The name 'Appalachian Spring' got attached to it some other way."

Jennifer wished she could think of something high and lofty to say about *her* favorite music, something that would impress Nola Mae. But Nola Mae always shut herself in her bedroom when Jennifer played her records. "That stuff gives me a headache," she'd complain.

Jennifer and Nola Mae shared their age—both twenty-four—their house, and their profession as teachers, but there the similarities ended. Jennifer was not as pretty as her housemate, nor as well-read and sophisticated. But then, she didn't have aspirations to be "somebody" like Nola Mae did.

Nola Mae spent a lot of time cultivating her good looks, her long wavy hair, and her polished, well-shaped fingernails. And while Jennifer was a faithful member of the Clevis Baptist Church, Nola Mae's religious exercises were done on the floor, rolling, stretching, groaning. Occasionally she even jogged, though never in town where she might be seen. Besides her penchant for classical music and good literature, Nola Mae fancied herself a connoisseur of art, a gourmet, and a political savant. She was particular about those she associated with, and had it not been a matter of economics, she certainly would not have lived with Jennifer.

The small house they rented was located on the edge of the town of Clevis, at the end of Hazel Lane, and a little way up a low hill flanked by rhododendron. Behind the house a grove of huge pine trees covered the top of the rise. From this spot Jennifer could watch the Carla River winding its way past town. She could also see the Potter's house halfway down Hazel Lane, and next door to that the house of the postmistress, Frieda Copp. And on beyond was where Hazel Lane met Jensen Road and became Main Street.

Jennifer loved the pine grove. It was a place to rest and think as she listened to the soughing wind in the pines overhead. A place to study. A place to escape the tensions of the shared bungalow down below.

And the scene there was tense. The rent on their house was reasonable when split between two people, but the house was small, with little privacy. Such a situation might have proved difficult even for two friends. For Jennifer and Nola Mae, it was a serious problem, one they dealt with by going their own way as much as possible. They seldom ate together and had little to say to one another beyond the necessary exchanges that are part of two people living together.

It was hard for Jennifer to accept this situation. She wanted to be friends with Nola Mae, not to be like her or to go places with her, but just to have a good relationship.

Jennifer did have one important attribute in Nola Mae's eyes, however: she wasn't afraid of mice. Her grandmother had passed along a special tolerance for the little creatures and the art of conversing with them.

Shortly after they moved in, Nola Mae was in the pantry closet checking out the storage potential when she opened a drawer, screeched, and ran hysterically into her bedroom. Jennifer couldn't get her calmed down enough to find out what was wrong, so she peered cautiously into the closet and saw the open drawer.

"Oh! They're so cute! Come look at them, Nola Mae. There are five babies."

Strangled sounds came from the bedroom.

Jennifer poked at the fluffy mass where the adult mice were hiding, and they darted behind some styrofoam cups, unwilling to abandon their little ones. "Come on now—you know you can't stay here. Why don't you take your babies out and put them under the porch? Oh, you probably wouldn't do that; you'd pick Nola Mae's bedroom." She chuckled to herself, then called, "Nola Mae, open the side door and I'll put them outdoors."

"No! I won't go anywhere near them!"

"Just open the door. Then you can get out of the way."

Nola Mae crept out and pushed open the door, still shuddering.

Jennifer removed the drawer carefully, carried it outside, and left it on the ground. Within an hour the mice were gone, and after Jennifer had washed out the drawer, Nola Mae finally stopped pacing and shivering.

Not long after that, Raskolnikov came to live with them. Rusty Chisholm mentioned to Jennifer that he had taken in a stray cat, but his mom didn't want it around. Jennifer talked it over with Nola Mae, who quickly decided that the problems of having a cat were preferable to having mice.

At that time Nola Mae was absorbed in things Russian, so they named the cat Raskolnikov. He was a good mouser, and except for the few times when they unwittingly let him in with mouse in tow, Nola Mae was quite happy

11

with the arrangement. And Jennifer was content with this first small step toward better relations.

2 Clevis. A small town where everybody knew everybody else. So small that it was purely due to geography that there was even a school in town. Foar's Knob, with its winding roads, especially treacherous in winter, was the reason the four-room elementary school hadn't been closed and consolidated with the Jensen school system. High school students rode the bus to Jensen, at least when the roads were navigable, but the Clevis school still served the younger children from Clevis, Plum, Dorsil, and the mountainous area beyond Plaggett Knob.

Jensen was the town of note in the area, complete with newspaper, lawyer, hospital, movie theater, and bowling alley. But because of the mountain, the nine-mile trip from Clevis to Jensen was not made lightly. Indeed, with the nearest doctor located in Jensen, long-time Clevis folk regularly included in their prayers the request that they not be injured or fall ill during a winter storm.

The town of Clevis was basically just one road that went somewhere. It came over the mountain from Jensen and went on to Plum where it intersected Plaggett Road. The other two roads that went out of town, Elm and Melon, turned to dirt and ended in a couple of barnyards back in the hills. The closest bridge across the Carla River was in Plum, there being only a foot ford in Clevis. A triangle of streets—Main, Elm, and Maple—formed the center of town, and along these streets were found most of the important Clevis establishments—the church and cemetery, the school, library, post office, hardware and drug stores, and Smith's General Store.

But how does a newcomer meet a town? Does she stand in front of the post office and shout, "I'm Jennifer Darrow. How do you do?" And to which part of town does she direct her query—the buildings, the people, or the social structures? Does a town have a personality, emotions, a smell even? What stories are hidden away in those little modules of living space, and how do these affect the composite disposition of the town?

The town VIPs had made their presence known to Jennifer soon after her arrival. Miss Sadie McCusker was of old Clevis stock, her forebears going back to pre-Civil War days before West Virginia became a separate state. Her large sycamore-shaded house on the corner of Main Street and Maple Avenue had never been without a McCusker in residence, but future prospects for the family line looked dim. Miss Sadie had taught in Clevis for many years and still substituted occasionally, but Jennifer learned from Nola Mae that because of Miss Sadie's rigid old-line strictness, she was at the bottom of everyone's list.

Lietta Wickens, the starchy librarian, was likewise well-rooted in Clevis. It was due to her interest and money that the town even had a library, and she fostered many of the social and political events of the town.

Hubert Smith and his wife Hilda were pillars of a different sort. As proprietors of Smith's General Store, they were in a good position to keep a close watch on church and town events, as well as any potential threats to local patriotism. Their chief thorn in the flesh, however, was having to live directly across from the Reggis family with their brood of dirty, foul-mouthed girls, their furniture-slinging fights, and worst of all, Jake's government pension for an army-related injury which, according to Hubert, was as phony as a liberal's promise.

The Reggis family was low on the social scale of Clevis, but they were at least noticed. Not hidden and secluded on the far edge of town like Galina Kostyukov, a shy Russian immigrant whose American husband had abandoned her to survive as best she could on her truck garden and pottery.

These people, then, the great and the small, were part of the fabric of Clevis, but on the whole, the community boasted no one of substantial note, had made no great historical mark. It was an insignificant town by a minor river in the remote hill country of West Virginia where, as the state motto proclaimed, "Mountaineers Are Always Free."

Yet Jennifer Darrow had come here to live and work, knowing she had only two initial points of contact, the school—and Corey.

The Clevis school was a strictly utilitarian, one-story brick structure built in the late 1940s after the old frame building had burned down. Behind the school a wooded hill rose and went on down to Jensen Road. Another smaller hill lay between the school and Main Street. Between the two wound a footpath, a shortcut from Hazel Lane that Jennifer usually took.

The school boasted no particular distinction in either facilities or faculty. Besides Jennifer, who taught the third and fourth grades, there was Nola Mae for the seventh and eighth grades; Mrs. Hedgley, a warm, motherly, but otherwise unremarkable woman, for the first and second grades; and Mrs. Sabre, the principal, who taught the fifth and sixth grades and lived in Plum. Assorted aides, lunch people, itinerant art and music teachers, and medical people came and went. And, of course, there was Jeremy Thurston Tybolt, the County Superintendent of Schools, who stopped by occasionally, usually at lunchtime so he could eat with Nola Mae.

Jennifer's class was small. Even with two grades, there were only seventeen students in her room. It was a relatively tranquil group, with almost twice as many girls as boys. An ideal class, Jennifer thought, so different from her classes of the previous two years. She often wondered how students in the city school would have reacted to Rosalie. Would they have tormented her, or would she have won them over with her lovable nature? Jennifer was glad she didn't have to find out.

Rosalie was *special* in every sense of the word. On the first day of school, Jennifer had greeted her in sign language with, "Hello, I'm your teacher, Miss Darrow." Rosalie, deaf since the age of three, threw her arms around Jennifer and laughed and jumped up and down at the prospect of real communication. Her new teacher "spoke" her language.

Rosalie was a delightful child—slender, with a delicate, transparent beauty. Jennifer found her happy, loving, curious, lively, and a quick learner. She exhibited few of the psychological or social handicaps that a condition such as deafness usually brings. Most of the school children liked her and teased her only minimally, which she usually handled by making a face and laughing at herself. Once in a great while, however, Rosalie would go off in a corner by herself and either cry or make a big pile of whatever was at hand, books or rocks or single blades of grass. It usually came after a music session or a joke that no one had thought to explain to her. But this was rare. She seemed to have an innate courage that refused self-pity and made the best of what she had.

A leader among her close friends Cindy Lindel and Selena Reggis, Rosalie often had them jumping rope or playing house or collecting leaves according to her directives. These girls knew best how to "talk" with her, but the other children had picked up enough, especially after

Jennifer's arrival, to be able to communicate to some degree. Being one of the mountain children, Rosalie relished the social opportunities that school afforded and made the most of her friendships.

Jennifer found advantages to sign language, especially in providing private conversations. She sometimes used this privacy to talk to Rosalie about Jesus. Normally she wouldn't have done this during school hours, but Rosalie would raise the subject, and Jennifer could see no harm in discussing it, just as she would any other matter that arose. Rosalie knew about Christmas and Easter and, most of all, that Jesus loved her. She could even sing "Jesus Loves Me," though it resembled more the call of a mourning dove than the familiar tune. Jennifer determined to ask Rosalie's father about that someday. She knew the child's mother had died a few years ago. She must have been a remarkable and devout woman to instill such a positive outlook in one so young.

This was Jennifer's first year of teaching in Clevis, and Corey had helped her get the job. She had been teaching in Philadelphia and wasn't happy, so when he called to tell her about the two vacancies in the Clevis school, she applied immediately. Many others had applied also, some fresh out of college and therefore less expensive to hire, but Jennifer had an asset Corey stressed to good effect in his role as her representative. In college, she had roomed with a deaf girl and had acquired considerable skill in using sign language. Thus, with the need in Clevis for such a skill, Jennifer was hired.

When Corey went to such lengths to get her here, Jennifer began dreaming. The two had been good friends in college and had corresponded some since then, but this unexpected turn of events had interesting possibilities. She pictured herself as a pastor's wife, standing at the rear of Clevis Baptist Church at the close of a service beside tall, blond, handsome Corey Witham. Rev. and Mrs. Corey Witham . . .

Although they had dated in college, Corey had been too well-disciplined to get involved with a girl before his long-range schedule permitted, so they were simply good friends. They shared a love for gospel music, particularly country gospel, and often went to concerts together. Corey played guitar, and they would sing together by the hour.

There was less time for that now, of course, but Corey did take time to help Jennifer get settled in and make her feel welcome in the community and in the church. He had been in Clevis himself only since the previous spring, but he had already charmed his way into the hearts of the church folk. And when Jennifer came along in late August, she was certain that people viewed her in a better light because she knew Corey.

Corey actually served two churches, common practice in small rural parishes. The other church was in Dorsil, along with the parsonage. Dorsil was a smaller town than Clevis, about seven miles west and away from the river.

Away from the river. Jennifer wouldn't be happy about that. Already she loved the Carla, especially the sound of its rushing waters deep in the gorge. In the middle of town, where the banks were much lower and the water smoother, there were several huge, flat stones for crossing the river when the water was low enough. Jennifer loved to stand on these rocks in the middle of the river, the words of one of Nola Mae's favorite songs running through her head: "Waters ripple and flow, slowly passes each day . . . ." She couldn't remember the rest, something about faithless lovers, turning mountains, and freedom, but the music sounded ripply, just like the Carla.

No, she wouldn't like leaving the river, but the parsonage would be considerably larger than the house at the end of Hazel Lane. And Corey would be there.

17

3   Corey Witham bounded up the steps of Smith's General Store. He had first walked from the church to Miss Sadie McCusker's house to pick up copies of the minutes of a Missions Committee meeting and then across the street to give them to Hilda Smith for distribution among committee members. Miss Sadie's promptness in getting out reports was legendary, right in line with Corey's own *modus operandi*. He wanted to be sure the committee members received the report as soon as possible, hoping this would help to more speedily implement the committee's decisions.

But Hilda was busy with a customer, and her husband Hubert greeted him instead. "Mornin', Reverend. Fine day, ain't it, praise the Lord!"

"Good morning, Hubert. I was sorry you couldn't make it to the meeting last night. Hilda said you weren't feeling well."

"Well, ah—yes! That's right. Not feeling well. A touch o' dyspepsy, I think. What can I do for you, Reverend? Some groceries this morning?"

"No, I just need to talk with Hilda a few moments, so I'll wait till she's free."

The store, a ramshackle building with a wavy wood-plank floor that meandered to various aisles and nooks, offered an assortment of groceries, housewares, dry and yard goods, shoes and clothing. It was a rather dreary place with long reaches of dusty clutter, except for one small corner just inside the front door. The Firemen's Auxiliary rented this spot for a weekly bake sale, and the ladies had cleaned and fancied up the window with hanging

18

plants and decorative items. Crafts of all kinds were big in the area, and even though Main Street, Clevis, was not exactly a major tourist route, word got around, and that little corner became a mecca of sorts for knowledgeable buyers. Galina for one was able to sell a substantial portion of her lovingly made pottery right there.

This pleasant entryway, then, served to draw people into the store, and since there was little competition, the Smiths enjoyed a rather brisk trade.

Hilda was waiting on Wesley Bishop, the barber, a rangy, slack-jawed fellow whose heart was set on Nola Mae. He wanted to buy candy for her but couldn't decide what kind. Chocolates were, of course, his first choice, but he ruminated aloud that they might cause her to break out in pimples. Next among his own favorites was peanut butter fudge, but again he shook his head. What if she had dentures? There were caramels—no, they were sticky, too. He scratched his head in bewilderment.

In the produce department—one table with some rather limp-looking lettuce, peppers, and celery—Corey met Ellen Lindel with four-year-old Kevin in tow.

"How are you, Ellen? Hey there, Kevin!" The lad stared solemnly and silently up at the tall figure standing before him.

"I'm glad I bumped into you, Ellen. I wanted to find out what you folks decided at your teachers' meeting the other night. I meant to call yesterday but ran out of day before I could get to it. And—" he glanced over at Wesley, still shifting indecisively from one foot to the other, "it looks as though Hilda will be tied up for a while. Do you have a minute?"

Ellen followed his glance and chuckled. "Yes . . . poor Wes! He's set his sights pretty high this time."

"A girl?"

"Mm, Nola Mae. Hasn't Jennifer told you?"

Corey shook his head incredulously, at the same time feeling several tugs on his suit jacket. *"He's buying candy for Nola Mae? Is he out of his mind?"*

"Yes, I think he is, just a bit." Ellen looked at the barber pityingly. "But at least he's buying candy and not drowning his sorrows at Tully's Lounge."

Corey frowned, and the tugs continued. "He shouldn't be wasting time and money on a worldly woman like her. Does she give him any encouragement?"

"Nola Mae? She'd sooner encourage a snake!"

Corey looked down as the persistent tugs finally registered. "Yes, Kevin, what is it?"

The small boy dropped his hand and looked at Corey with large, serious eyes. "Are you God?"

Ellen laughed merrily. "Oh, Kevin! Of course not!"

But Corey put his hand on the boy's shoulder and responded as seriously as asked. "No, son, I'm not God. You see me in God's house and hear me speak God's Word, and I can understand how you might be confused. We can't see God with our eyes, but we know what He's like from reading the Bible. Do your mommy and daddy read the Bible to you?"

Kevin nodded solemnly.

"When you grow up and can read it by yourself, you'll come to know and love God, too. He loves you very much, you know. Now, if you'll excuse us, your mother and I have some other things to talk about."

Corey and Ellen went on to discuss the Christian Education meeting, Corey keeping an eye on Wesley's progress. He appeared to have narrowed the choice down to two possibilities: after-dinner mints, which were neither chocolate nor sticky and had the added advantage of smelling good should Nola Mae reward his beneficence with a kiss; and sour balls. The latter would last longer than any other kind he could think of, and after some rapid mental calculating he decided that they were by far the better bargain. "Why, with this whole bag o' sour balls, she'll think o' me at least five hunnert minnits, 'stead o' jist a few!" So with a seraphic smile and sigh of satisfaction, he paid his eighty-nine cents and headed for the door.

Corey called after him. "See you tonight at the fire station, Wes?"

"Yessir, Rev! I'll be there with th' boys!"

Corey finished his discussion with Ellen and then turned to Hilda for the Missions Committee business. As he did, Kevin turned a dazzling smile on him and waved a warm goodbye.

The fire station at the east end of Laurel Road was a social mecca for the seventeen volunteer firemen, plus a few others like Hubert Smith who dropped in on occasion just for the camaraderie. They spent many hours polishing their two small fire trucks, not impressive in themselves but objects of great community pride. These trucks served the area from Foar's Knob to Dorsil and Plaggett Knob, and they were occasionally called on to help the local forest fire control units.

The fire station was a two-stall cement-block structure with a large room on the second floor for meetings and other gatherings. The shiny fire pole was an unessential embellishment but the joy of every Clevis youngster allowed to enter the building. Not all were; the men were careful about who they trusted around their trucks and on the pole.

Of the seventeen men, only a few were active members of the Clevis Baptist Church, and only Randy Lindel was more apt to be found at church affairs than at firehouse poker games. But Pastor Corey treated them all with equal friendliness when he dropped in from time to time. Because he joked and bantered more than preached, the men didn't mind his presence. They did feel constrained to clean up their language and stories a bit, but they weren't about to pour their beer down the floor drain, and Corey felt at ease with them. He had sensitivity and a special ability for talking with people about spiritual matters without buttonholing them. He cared about the needs of others, and the men respected and listened to him. He did use these contacts as a base for one-on-one evangelism in other contexts, but at the firehouse he was relaxed and affable, and the men happily bestowed on him the informal status of Fire Chaplain.

Corey liked that and treated it seriously. He didn't help out at fires—he would only have been a hindrance anyway—but was on call to give aid and comfort any time he was needed.

These contacts, then, between firemen and chaplain were agreeable to the men, and kingdom business to Corey. He understood the significance of their acceptance of him, but he was not there for fun and games nor for any social benefit that might accrue.

But rewards of another kind did issue from his time spent with the men. Though Corey had been blessed with the gift of evangelism, his mechanical aptitude was nonexistent, and he couldn't even put a quart of oil in his car unaided. He had learned to pump gas for himself, but even there his first try in Charleston had required a ten-minute instructional session over the intercom with the hermetically sealed Self-Serv attendant. He was as helpless under the hood of a car as a newly hatched tadpole, and the men took it upon themselves to bail him out when things went wrong, which happened frequently. It became a game for them to try to determine from his vague descriptions just what the problem was. They did their best by him, and Corey was not ungrateful, though it *was* hard for him to say so.

4 September was a beautiful month for Jennifer to explore her new environment. She loved the outdoors, and as often as she could, she walked around town, stopping to chat with people as they picked tomatoes or watered flowers. Everyone knew who she was, so making new friends wasn't hard. She wished she could get Corey to walk with her, especially to some of the more remote areas. For instance, she wanted very much to explore a trail that went up along the gorge on the other side of the river. But Corey's regimen did not include walking simply for enjoyment, so she had to content herself with checking out on her own the streets and paths in town.

The change from city to country was for Jennifer a heady thing. Though she had spent most of her adult life in or near large cities, her heart found in Clevis the inner space that was best afforded by a rural environment.

And so that first month she took full advantage of the gorgeous weather to be outside as much as possible. The oppressive heat was past, and although a bit too dry for the gardeners, it was just fine for rambling or even doing schoolwork up in the pine grove.

She loved that spot. The pine trees filled the air with their incense, and the view, though not like being on top of a mountain, was a restful distraction from her daily responsibilities. Hardly anyone else went there. Nola Mae certainly didn't, Ed Potter went up once or twice a year to get needles for his strawberry bed. And occasionally Jennifer's friend Ellen Lindel would go there to put some psychological miles between herself and the children and her husband's store. For Jennifer, however, it became a retreat, a place to look out on the world or into her own heart. And sometimes it was just a place to lie and dream. Or to pour out a bit of time as a thank offering, much as David poured out the water brought to him from the well at Bethlehem.

But concentration on schoolwork was sometimes hard. Especially the day Grandpa Potter was out painting. He had six old-fashioned wooden lawn chairs which he kept in beautiful condition, and that week he had been painting one or two at a time. This particular day, Jennifer watched as he did the last one and touched up another. They were all grouped invitingly under the ash tree and looked splendid. After a final satisfied inspection, he went into the house to put away his painting equipment and came out fifteen minutes later with the newspaper and a tall glass in his hand. Jennifer watched in utter fascination as he settled himself—in the wrong chair! He sat for a moment as though turned to stone, then pulled himself up, his clothes sticking with great determination to the chair, and stalked back into the house with stately dignity.

But the lure of that trail across the river tugged at Jennifer. Finally she asked Ed about it, and he assured her that if she kept the river in sight, she couldn't possibly get lost.

So Corey or no, Jennifer decided one particularly beautiful Saturday morning to pack a lunch and go exploring. She left the house determined to savor every step of the way and drew in refreshing gulps of crisp air that held in suspension all the ripe fullness of summer's end. Heavy scents: ripe apples, wild grapes, and late tomatoes. Rich colors: goldenrod, blue asters, and changing leaves. Overhead, starlings in ballet choreography, wheeling and turning in perfect unity.

The Carla was unusually low, and the fording stones were more than a foot out of the water. On the far side, Jennifer had to clamber through a patch of innocent-looking weeds that left little forked prickers all over her jeans. She stopped a moment to pull them off and was startled by the rattling cry of a scruffy-looking bird as it flew down river. She was surprised at how different the river looked from this side. She wished Corey was with her, but then, he wouldn't know any more than she what flowers and trees and birds they were looking at. How could a person be so totally disinterested in everything outdoors? He didn't even like picnics. "Too many bugs!" he would say.

With a final brush to her jeans, Jennifer moved along the trail and soon came to a path that went off to the left. A holly tree marked the junction, almost as though it had been planted there for that purpose. That would be the trail up Sugar Hill, where the Clevis Baptist Church held its Easter sunrise service. And from what Ed Potter had said, most of the able-bodied townsfolk made their way up each year.

The trail along the river was steep, but Jennifer moved along slowly, looking and smelling and savoring under the hardwood canopy.

While inspecting several tall, white, umbrella-like toadstools, she heard a noise close by. She rose quietly, expecting to see a squirrel but hoping it might be something larger. As she tiptoed up the trail, a man stepped from behind a rhododendron-skirted hemlock and blocked her way. Jennifer gave a sharp cry and jumped back, then laughed weakly, trying to collect herself.

"You scared me! I didn't see you coming. I thought it was a squirrel . . ." her voice trailed off as surprise gave way to fear. This was no ordinary person, one who would politely tip his hat and pass on with a pleasant "Good morning." This man was clearly Trouble.

He was tall, over six feet, and well-proportioned, but his long dark hair and beard had seen neither soap nor comb in months. His soft leather shirt, jeans, and boots—though obviously good quality—were stained and dirty.

But most terrifying to her was the cold, leering smirk on his face. When he spoke, his tone was soft but menacing.

"Th' new schoolmarm, I b'lieve. How-dee-do?" *How does he know who I am?* Jennifer thought. *What should I do now?* She was trembling, but decided to respond as casually as possible to his mock politeness.

"Yes, I am new in town. I don't believe I've met you."

He laughed. "Guess maybe you'd remember if you hed. An' I reckon you'll hear plenty 'bout me afore long, if they ain't a'ready told you." He leaned back against the hemlock. "Th' townfolk treatin' you okay? Hain't ben a-sceerin' you with fearful boogie-man tales, have they?" He frowned in mocking concern.

Jennifer knew he was toying with her, but it seemed best to keep the same light vein and hope to get away as soon as possible.

She smiled brightly. "Oh, no. They've been just wonderful, very kind and helpful." *Why didn't someone warn me about you?* she thought.

"How're you a-gittin' along with yer roommate? She brung home any stray dogs 'r cats—'r men? She's a lulu, ain't she? But a good teacher . . . you keep livin' with her, an' you'll larn a few tricks." Jennifer's eyes widened at his knowledge of her life and she could feel herself becoming more and more flustered.

"But then, you c'd prob'ly teach her a few things yerself. You got thet preacher a-buzzin' round ya. Or has he got you a–buzzin' round him? From what I unnerstand, he brung you here t' keep him warm them long, cold nights this winter."

26

At that, Jennifer wheeled to walk away, but with one stride he caught her arm and spun her around.

"Whoa! I ain't through yet, an' it ain't perlite t' trot away like that." His eyes flashed with anger, belying the lightness of his words.

He glowered at her a moment and then unleashed such a torrent of profanity and obscene innuendo that Jennifer was too startled and frightened to take it in. The intent was clear enough, though, and it meant danger. But when he started suggesting that she had come out just to meet someone, the preacher perhaps, or maybe even him, anger overrode her fear. She straightened and faced him squarely.

"Now look, Mr. whatever-your-name-is, I don't know who you are or why you're saying all these hateful things. You know as well as I that they're all lies, and you're just being—" she couldn't think of a strong enough word "—*hateful!*"

He smiled again and leaned back against the tree. "Well! Th' preacher's woman's got some spunk after all! You git that a-teachin' them puppies at the church? Some o' them boys must give you a purty warm time, Rusty and his pals."

Again the thought ran through her mind: *How does he know so much about me and what I do?* Then, in both fear and anger she blurted out, "I'm not afraid of you! You can say all the nasty things you want, but the Lord is my defender and protector."

Leaning against the tree with arms folded, he laughed with malignant glee. "Oh? . . . That so?" Suddenly he straightened and lunged as though to grab her. Jennifer screamed and fled in terror back down the trail, his cruel laughter ringing in her ears.

She ran without stopping until she reached the river. In her haste to get across, she slipped off a rock and plunged one foot into the river before regaining her balance. She was

27

sobbing uncontrollably by the time she reached the other side, and after looking back to be sure he wasn't following, she collapsed into the safety of a rhododendron thicket.

She was angry with herself for having reacted like a scared rabbit when in effect all he did was say "Boo!" How hollow her brave words sounded in her ears! The Lord her defender and protector. Well, she *had* gotten away safely. She reconstructed the scene the way it might have been: he turning on her, she standing unflinching, quoting Bible verses, he falling back in chagrin and confusion, she making her retreat with great dignity before he had a chance to regroup. No, she thought sadly, she shouldn't have run; she was nothing but an object of scorn and derision in his eyes now. But did it really matter what a man like that thought of her?

Drawing a shaky breath, she smoothed her hair, brushed off her clothes, and pulled herself up the steep bank and headed toward Main Street. She was glad to see Hilda Smith out sweeping the porch, but as she sat on the wicker chair that Hilda offered, she began crying again in spite of herself, and the whole story came pouring out.

"Oh, my dear! What a terrible thing! What did he look like? Big an' dark an' dirty? An' was he wearin' sort of a fancy tan shirt, chamois, with braid or somethin' like it?"

"Yes . . . I think so. He was dirty, all right. And he had dark, bushy hair—sort of like Samson might have looked."

Hilda nodded grimly. "Uh-hm. Sounds like Tikki Granger all right."

"Who's he?"

"A terrible bad man! He hasn't been around fer awhile—comes an' goes when he feels like it, an' I haven't seen 'im most all summer. Thought maybe we'd got rid of 'im fer good."

"What does he do when he is around?"

Hilda became upset as she answered. "He mostly hangs

28

around Tully's an' stirs up all kinds of mischief, that's what he does! I don't know why he hasn't been locked up long before this. He's a menace to ev'ry man, woman, and child walkin' th' streets!" She got up and went over to Jennifer. "You sure you're all right, child? He didn't do nothin' to you? You was certainly lucky. My lands! . . .Can I git you a cup o' tea, honey? He's wicked—*wicked!*"

By now she was pacing and so agitated that Jennifer became alarmed once again. Perhaps she should report the incident to Ray Windle, Clevis's lone police officer. Even allowing for Hilda Smith's tendency to overreact, there seemed to be something about this Tikki Granger that was genuinely upsetting to her.

"Has he always lived around here?" Jennifer asked.

"He don't live here a'tall. Sometimes he stays with some of the good-fer-nothin's around town, but mostly he's up in the mountains, prob'ly plottin' more deviltry. He hasn't always been here, just the past ten years or so. That's why I think he's some kind of agitator or somethin'."

Just then Ellen Lindel came by on her way home from town, and Hilda called to her in her loudest, most piercing tone. "Ellen! Did y' hear what happened t' Jennifer? Tikki Granger got aholt of her an' nearly raped her!" Jennifer cringed and knew right then that she should call Corey as soon as she got home so he would hear the story straight. By the time Hilda got through with it, any resemblance to fact would be purely coincidental.

As soon as they could break away, the two young women walked on down to Ellen's small but neat house at the foot of Hazel Lane, and Jennifer accepted her friend's invitation to share a bit of lunch.

The three Lindel children had already eaten and left a mess. Ellen sighed and called them to clean it up. She said little to Jennifer while the youngsters were banging and arguing at their chores, but after they had gone back to their game and she had set some soup and cornbread on the table, she began to talk about Tikki Granger.

"As far as I know, Jennifer, he's never done anything that actually *harmed* anyone. Ray Windle has talked to him many times, but no matter how strongly implicated he is in trouble, there's just no way to prove he's guilty of any wrongdoing. He's either careful not to become personally involved or clever enough not to get caught. But I'm scared to death that someday he'll flip out and really do some damage. I worry most about the children . . . what he might do to them. You hear so many horrible stories nowadays, and if he *is* unbalanced, he could be a disaster just waiting to happen." She stared unseeing out the window, hearing in a special way Kevin's indignant protest over his older siblings' game tactics.

"Does he treat everyone like he treated me? Talk to them in that horrible way?" Jennifer asked.

"There are some he gets along with better than others, let's put it that way. He and Kenny Stuckworth are pretty thick. Tikki sometimes stays in the old shack way in behind Kenny's place. He and Kenny and Joey Hamlin—they're the main troublemakers."

Jennifer thought a few moments, then said, "Hilda sure got upset when she was talking about him."

"Oh, yes!" Ellen laughed. "It wasn't amusing at all to them, and I try to keep a straight face when they talk about it, but it *was* funny. It happened late last spring.

"Hubert went in the store one morning and found almost every can on the shelves turned upside down. He checked the doors and windows but couldn't find any sign of a break-in. He reported it to Ray, who said he'd keep an eye on the place.

"A few days later, the same thing happened. Only this time things were rearranged. Shoes in the meat case. Hu's right-wing magazines under the counter. And women's

30

colored underpants wired into a bouquet in the Auxiliary corner. It really was funny.

"Well, Hubert decided to stay all night in the store and keep watch himself. He didn't really expect anything to happen while he was there, at least not the first night, but somehow they got in without him knowing. Then they waited till he went to the bathroom and locked him in!"

"Locked him in the *bathroom?*" Jennifer laughed.

"In the bathroom! There was just one window, but Hu could never have squeezed through it, so he just sat there till Hilda came in the morning!"

The two girls laughed uproariously at the imagined scene. "Better than being locked *out!*" added Jennifer. "But how do you lock someone in a bathroom?"

"Oh! I forgot the funniest part! Apparently, one of them held the door shut while the others pushed a large display shelf against the door. Then they slipped a note under the door, saying that every piece of expensive glassware in the store was on those shelves, so if he pushed the door too hard, it would all be broken. And just for effect, they broke a piece of glass on the floor before they left."

Jennifer shook her head admiringly. "Who has all the brains in that group—Tikki? Certainly not Kenny or Joey!"

"Oh, Tikki's smart, all right! He's sometimes called 'The Fox' and with good cause. But the best part is, when Hilda got to the store in the morning, there wasn't a *thing* on the shelves. They were bare! It was all a bluff!"

Jennifer went home feeling considerably better than when she had stumbled across the river. But even laughing with Ellen couldn't erase the memories of terror that rose up within her when she thought of the repulsive mountain man.

5 Corey wasn't as upset as Jennifer thought he might be. He expressed concern, of course, but after being assured that she was all right, he simply cautioned her against wandering off again alone.

Corey had heard of Tikki but hadn't met him. Jennifer thought Corey might feel a little apprehensive at the prospect, but he told her that when the time came, he'd know how to handle it. And in the meantime, why worry about it?

And Corey would handle it well, Jennifer thought. He was so self-assured that little bothered him. Never afraid, he said what he needed to with straightforward firmness and left people with the impression that he was fully in control.

Jennifer tried to picture the two men together—Corey and Tikki. They were about the same height, but Corey was more slender, almost fine-boned. Corey was blond, Tikki dark. And Tikki's uncouthness and vulgarity were a stark contrast to Corey's smooth talk and polished manner. Light and dark, day and night, oil and—well—*muddy* water. How would they react to each other if and when they met? She rather hoped she wouldn't be on hand for Tikki's inevitable remarks about the preacher and his "woman."

She was glad Corey wasn't bothered by the insinuations in such remarks. He knew in his own mind what he was, and criticism just rolled off him. Jennifer felt safe with Corey, knowing that most people liked and respected him and therefore tended to like and respect her as well. She, who had never been socially prominent, suddenly felt elevated to the more privileged class of Being Noticed, and it was pleasant. She tried not to take advantage of her friendship with Corey or to make it bear more freight than it should at this point, but it was fun to be the subject of approving looks and comments when she was with him.

She sensed that Corey liked being seen with her, too. Though busy with two churches, he often took her out to dinner or to a gospel concert, even as far away as Charleston. He also made time just to be with her to talk. He liked to bounce ideas off her, he said, and he was very patient in trying to get her to see the rightness of his position on any issue. But he never took her to the parsonage in Dorsil unless other people were present. When they were together in Clevis, it was usually in the library or at Cooper's luncheonette and ice cream shop. That is not to say they were never alone or that they didn't enjoy being alone. The discovery that she was being actively courted pleased and flattered Jennifer, and she *did* enjoy it, but in her security she also enjoyed controlling the relationship from being pushed along too fast.

Corey was goal-oriented. In addition to his unspoken aim of finding a wife in a year's time, he also wanted to build up the youth program of the Clevis and Dorsil churches. When he first came, the teenagers had no Sunday school nor youth activities of any kind. In fact, very few teenagers even went to church. And if they had, it is doubtful anyone would have been willing to work with them. Corey was determined to change this, and as soon as Jennifer arrived, he enlisted her as leader of the Clevis youth group, giving her three weeks to prepare for the first meeting.

That meeting went quietly enough, with Carol Stanley, a shy, pretty girl of fifteen, and Hubie Smith, a fat and rather lazy lad of fifteen, being the only young people to show up. The next week, however, reaped the fruit of

33

Corey's efforts, with Betsy Sabre, a lively, vivacious four-teen-year-old coming from Plum, and fifteen-year-old Rusty Chisholm, coming because Betsy came. That meeting was more of a challenge, but nothing compared to the following week. In addition to the four of the previous week, there were three young people from Dorsil, plus Brian Cooper and John Considine (known as Coop and Connie) from Clevis, and Rolanda and Daphne, two of the six Reggis girls. Corey had another meeting that evening and couldn't be there to help, and Jennifer felt she had been thrown to the wolves. It was total disaster from her point of view. The kids didn't know any of the songs she had chosen and wouldn't have sung anyway under any conditions. Her carefully planned progression into what she thought would be an interesting Bible study quickly ran aground when the kids began chasing each other around the room, heaving chairs behind to trip up their pursuers. Even after she managed to get them seated, they joked and giggled, some making obscene gestures. Obviously a Bible study that evening was impossible. She gave up, sent them all home, and waited in misery for Corey.

As usual, he listened patiently and sympathetically to her review of the whole wretched experience, but wouldn't hear of her suggestion that he find someone else for the job. He promised to help her plan future meetings and to see that another adult was always on hand if he was not available.

The church's youth program was very important to Corey, almost a symbol of his effectiveness as a minister to reach not just the old folks, who would probably have gone to church if Wesley Bishop had been the preacher, but also the young people. He knew it wouldn't be easy, especially given his decision that from the very start someone other than himself would actually run the show. He would be right there, of course, to help and encourage as

34

a good administrator, but Jennifer was the one through whom he would work.

Corey ran a tight ship, laying down clear ground rules prohibiting alcohol, cigarettes, drugs, swearing, and even dancing, card-playing, and movies. He set out for Jennifer the subjects to be covered during the year, many based on his list of taboos, and helped her develop a program that would attract the teenagers in the area.

Not being a person given to frivolity, Corey found it difficult to allow for the kind of nonsense and play that teens thrive on, but he figured it in as a necessary ingredient to seeing his goal achieved. Without fail, he did a post-mortem with Jennifer on how the planned foolishness had gone over each week and how well it had helped carry out the night's theme.

After Jennifer began to learn the ways and wiles of teenagers, the meetings went reasonably well, especially if Coop and Connie stayed away. Even with Corey on hand, they were a problem. They openly admitted they were there for fun and girls and not because of any spiritual interests. They bent every rule as far as they could without getting bounced out the door, and occasionally, if things weren't lively enough to suit them, they did something outrageous just to get themselves tossed out.

Jennifer felt particularly discouraged after nights like that. The boys had grown up next door to each other and thought alike, but she couldn't help wondering how much tutoring they were getting on the side from Tikki Granger. Some of their tricks clearly bore his trademark. Once they inserted pornographic flyers in every Bible they could lay their hands on, including the big one on the pulpit. Another time, during group prayer, they began murmuring "A-men! Hallelujah! Yes, Lord!" increasing their fervency till many in the group were shouting at the top of their lungs, and the whole thing broke down in hilarity.

Jennifer found, though, that good refreshments at the close of the meetings held a special power, not just for Coop and Connie but for all the kids. The mere threat of being excluded from the "eat beat" often held them in line when nothing else would. So Jennifer put extra effort into preparing special treats.

But from the kids' point of view, even the night Jennifer sent them all home was a success. They had fun and the meetings were for *them*, something that hadn't been true in the church since long before they had been teenagers.

Rusty, the young person most affected by the presence or absence of Coop and Connie, was both delight and grief for Jennifer. He was an irrepressible boy, scatterbrained and full of mischief, but he had a disarming smile that was his greatest personal asset in avoiding the consequences of his misdoings.

Wherever there were girls, there was Rusty. Clumsy and unpolished but ever amusing, he always managed to draw a satisfying amount of giggling attention. When with the Baptist girls, he was a model Baptist, singing lustily, parroting properly pious sentiments, causing Jennifer's hopes to soar. But he was easily led and influenced, and when his friends were on hand, he slipped into his Mr. Hyde character and threw all his energies into deviltry. Rusty rather admired Tikki Granger, "The Fox," and the mysterious intrigue surrounding him. When the latter was around town, the boy would plague him either by trying to play up to him or, when that didn't work, by stalking him and posturing behind his back. He tried very hard in his own inept way to get attention from the man, but Tikki seemed to ignore Rusty and his coltish ways much as a big dog might ignore a playful kitten.

But the dog could and did snap once in awhile. In early October the youth group was scheduled for a hayride in Virgil Hanover's mule-drawn wagon. Rusty, Coop, and

Connie left early to walk to Hanover's farm and at Rusty's suggestion went by way of Kenny Stuckworth's shack where Tikki was in residence at the moment. Rusty wanted to do a little prior boasting about his hayride conquests, but he happened on the bear at the wrong time. Tikki listened to his swagger for a moment, then grabbed him by the scruff of the neck. "I'll fix you up with somethin' real special t' hep you git on with them gurls," he growled and dragged him off, kicking and hollering, into the woods behind the shack. Coop and Connie, keeping a sober and respectful distance, watched as Tikki hauled him to a very dead and odorous skunk. He flipped him to the ground and proceeded to work him over from head to toe, rubbing the reeking carcass into his hair, skin, and clothing. Rusty wriggled and screamed and gagged but could do absolutely nothing about it until Tikki stuffed the remains down the boy's shirt and stalked off to his cabin. Coop and Connie crept off silently, thankful that they had been overlooked in the matter.

And so Rusty's saintliness had a slight momentary downswing while he quarantined himself from social contact, but he was soon back in full form, playing the girls and God on one hand, the boys and the Devil on the other. But during the sporadic spells when sainthood prevailed, Jennifer sometimes pondered the similarities between a dead skunk and the jawbone of an ass.

6   Jennifer offended Nola Mae Ramsey in three particular ways: first, Jennifer's friends; second, her cultural tastes; and third, everything else about her.

It wasn't that Nola Mae was disagreeable. In her own circle she was highly sought after—intelligent, witty, able to hold her own in almost any social gathering. The only thing she lacked was money, but she made judicious use of her small teacher's salary to maximize the outward appearance of her bank account.

She might have had more available cash had she been on better terms with her family, her father being one of the top executives in an electronics corporation. He had given her everything but himself, and it hadn't taken her long to identify her own sense of alienation with the evils of the capitalist system and move away from her parents' business-oriented conservatism to a more liberal posture.

Nola Mae was a peculiar mixture of aesthetic taste and petty ambition. She truly enjoyed fine literature and good music and bluntly rejected "trash" of any kind in the realm of music, theater, film, or television. She traveled to Charleston once a week to rehearse with the city choral society, though hers was not an outstanding voice. Art, on the other hand, was an area she had learned just enough about to bandy some jargon and to foster the illusion of expertise, but not enough to help her understand or enjoy it to any great extent.

She was an avid reader, at least when she could squeeze it into her busy schedule. Although particularly fond of poetry, she tried on principle to cover a broad spectrum of material, from Greek epics to nineteenth-century detective stories to modern philosophers. She was presently reading the works of Russian authors—Tolstoy, Dostoevsky, Chekhov, Solzhenitsyn—and listening to the music of Tchaikovsky, Stravinsky, and Khatchaturian.

This mixture of genuine appreciation for a wide variety of art forms and insensitive cultural snobbery explained why Nola Mae looked down on Jennifer's literary outlook. She sometimes dropped names like John Donne, George

Herbert, and William Blake, while laying a book on Jennifer's desk in an offhand way, saying, "You might like some of these poems."

Nola Mae was also ambitious. Not about her profession, although she was a reasonably capable teacher, but about carving a niche in the world that "mattered," as she put it. Clevis and its people did not matter to her. The other teachers in the school did not matter either; they were too ordinary and plodding to be of any use to her. And her lovelorn admirer, Wesley Bishop, certainly did not matter, despite his optimistic barbershop rhetoric.

One person who did matter and at whose behest she had taken the teaching position in Clevis was County Superintendent of Schools, Jeremy Thurston Tybolt. He was a young, handsome bachelor—and interested in Nola Mae. *And* he had connections. He lived in Jensen where he had a number of influential friends and also knew people in high places in Charleston.

So even though living on a dead-end street and teaching seventh and eighth grades in a backwater town, Nola Mae Ramsey considered herself in a good position indeed for furthering her goals and aspirations.

The immediate nuisance was having to put up with Jennifer. It wasn't Jennifer's clothes that bothered her so much, although their tastes ran in totally opposite directions. Nola Mae was "high fashion," whereas Jennifer wore puffy sleeves and lace and tiny-flower prints. No, it was the reason behind Jennifer's choice, at least as Nola Mae saw it. Jennifer took pains with her appearance because she was dating Corey. And Corey was the sore point with Nola Mae. She couldn't abide him, despite his good looks and immaculate grooming. To Nola Mae, Corey even smelled like a Baptist minister.

And in one way or another, possibly from only half-listening to Jennifer's account of Rusty and the skunk, Nola

Mae had gotten it fixed in her mind that Tikki Granger had some sort of connection with the church and Jennifer, which only increased her disdain for them all. If she had thought about it much or watched Jennifer shudder involuntarily at odd moments, she would have known it to be absurd.

But an incident occurred that only strengthened the notion.

It was late in October, the remaining russets, umbers, yellows and oranges forming an exquisite Persian rug tapestry against the mountainous backdrop of smoky purple and blue. Most of the rug, however, now lay flat on the ground after a day and a half of heavy rain. A cold, blustery front had come through, dropping the temperature down near freezing, with the wind chill considerably below that. Nola Mae had gone to Charleston for her Monday-evening choral rehearsal, so Jennifer was home alone, keeping the stove stoked and vacillating between correcting papers or working on lesson plans, when what she really wanted to do was curl up with an apple and a book.

The cat rambled aimlessly through the silent house, peering first into Nola Mae's darkened room at the left rear of the house, then into the bath that separated the two bedrooms. The door to the large walk-in pantry was closed against drafts, thus barring him from his food, so he poked about the kitchen area, a gloomy corner with a northern window that drew whatever light was available through the additional filter of the front porch. When his exploration took him to the table top and brought a sharp reprimand from Jennifer, he responded with a semi-argumentative meow and completed his circle by rubbing along her legs and hopping into her lap.

The small wood and coal stove on the west wall was doing a reasonable job of keeping the room warm, but Jennifer kept shivering, mostly from the roar of the wind and the rain-swollen river.

Just as she finally settled on doing the papers, leftovers from Friday, a noise on the front porch startled her. She first thought a tree had fallen on the house, but it wasn't loud enough for that. Had Nola Mae come home early for some reason? She got up and went to the door. There was someone on the porch, but she couldn't see well enough through the curtained window in the door to tell who it was.

She unlocked and opened the door—and gasped in frightened surprise. Tikki, soaking wet, shivering uncontrollably, and in obvious pain, leaned with outstretched arm against the house. He said nothing, just stood with head bent, looking ghastly. Despite Jennifer's initial inclination, she couldn't shut the door on him in that condition on this cold night, so she swallowed her fear and said in a shaky voice, "You're hurt . . . please . . . come in—what happened?"

Mumbling something about the river, he straightened with a grimace, came into the welcoming warmth of the living room, and lay down on the floor beside the stove. Jennifer knelt and put a hand on his shoulder, intending to find out where he was hurt and what she could do to help, but he shook her off and snarled at her to keep away, bringing more pain to himself in the process.

She stood back indecisively, chewing the side of her thumb, then went to the bathroom for a towel and to her closet for a blanket, knocking over a whole pile of boxes in her nervousness.

"You're soaking wet. Would you like to take your clothes off and wrap up in this blanket while they dry by the stove?" then bit her lip as she thought about the sound of that. But Tikki just shook his head and took the towel, sopping up some of the water from his head and arms. "Just a minute . . . I'll heat some soup."

A few minutes later, she approached him warily with a

warm mug, but he raised up on one elbow and accepted it, still shaking badly as he drank. She sat back on her heels for a moment, then got up and put another stick of wood in the stove. When he held out the empty cup, she noticed a long jagged scar at the base of his thumb. What sort of life had this man lived? And what was he doing on the floor of her living room?

"Would you like more? There's a bit left in the pan."

"No—it's enough." He lay back, eyes closed.

"I'll get you a pillow."

"No! Jes' leave me be!" He rolled over onto his stomach and shoved the partly folded towel under his head. Jennifer folded the blanket to double thickness for greater warmth and cautiously laid it over him. He didn't move. His tremors grew less and less, and within ten minutes he was asleep.

Jennifer sat quietly in her chair watching her mysterious guest. Why had Tikki come here? And what had happened to him? If he had fallen in the river at the ford, he had passed many other warm homes to come to her doorstep. Had she been foolish to let him in? Was he here for the night? What would Nola Mae say when she came home?

What *should* she do? Call Ray—or Corey? He might sleep through a quiet phone conversation, but she doubted it. He seemed to need sleep, and she didn't want to disturb him. But why did it matter that he not be disturbed? Maybe he had done something terrible and was running away when he fell in the river. Maybe he decided to hide out here where no one would think of looking for him.

But as Jennifer sat looking at the unconscious form on the floor, so vulnerable in weakness and sleep, it did matter that Tikki not be disturbed. By coming to her in this condition, he seemed to be saying that he trusted her. Something told her not to betray that trust.

After perhaps an hour had passed, with Jennifer distractedly working on her papers, Tikki rolled over with a groan and opened his eyes. She moved to the edge of her chair and waited, restraining herself from offering more soup. He looked around, saw her in the chair, but said nothing. He sat up gingerly and after a moment hauled himself to his feet, staggering and holding his head. There was a smear of blood on the towel where his head had rested. Jennifer's heart thumped wildly. What would he do or say next? What should she do now? But he simply opened the door, said, "Now you kin call Ray Windle like you bin a-wantin' to," and was gone.

Gone. Without even a remote thank you.

Should she call Ray? Or Corey? She rather thought not. One thing she was sure of: Corey would ask if she had witnessed to Tikki. Had she? Thinking back, she hadn't said much at all. She had asked him if he wanted to take his clothes off—she smiled at the idea of that being witnessing—given him soup and a blanket. Did that count? She thought so, but Corey probably wouldn't.

She was still mulling and pacing when Nola Mae got home at 11:30. Jennifer poured out the whole story, asking again the question she hadn't been able to get out of her mind: "Why, of all places, did he come here? Why not Smiths' or Lindels'? Joey Hamlin's apartment was right around the corner—why didn't he go there?"

But Nola Mae was tired and irritable, in no mood to speculate. "He came here because he's got you pegged as a soft touch. You and that church of yours are turning this place into a skid-row rescue mission. He knew you were the only person in town stupid enough not to slam the door and call Ray." Jennifer pondered whether that was good or bad.

And so, at a time when Jennifer badly needed a friend to

share her disquietude, she was locked out once again. Nola Mae had only enough friendliness for her own relatively small circle. Had she had more love from her father or been less of a striver for position, she might have been secure enough for that circle to take in one more; but as it was, Jennifer spent much of her time at home either physically or emotionally alone.

7 "Ellen, who am I?" Jennifer plopped down on her friend's couch as Ellen finished winding up the vacuum cord and took a final, wistful look around at the transitory neatness of her living room.

"Who are you?" She frowned in playful perplexity as she nodded them both toward the kitchen. "Let's see—Helen Keller, Madame Defarge, Scarlett O'Hara—who would you like to be?"

Jennifer laughed and filled the teakettle while Ellen stowed away the cleaning equipment. "I'd *like* to be Jennifer Darrow, thanks. It's about all I can handle right now, if I could just figure out who she is. You see," she settled into a chair, "in high school and college I thought I had myself pretty well figured out. I knew what I liked and what I wanted and thought it was just a matter of going out and putting it all into practice. But now I don't know. I'm one person when I'm with Corey and someone else when I'm teaching, and quite different still when I'm with you." She paused and chewed the side of her thumb. "Then there's Miss Sadie. She scares me half to death. Even when I just call her on the phone, I feel as though I should comb my hair. And with Nola Mae—" She frowned. "With Nola Mae, it's as though I'm—as though I don't exist. Less than a nobody."

"Who's that you're talking about?"

"Nola Mae."

"Who's she?" A smile played around Ellen's mouth as she set out the mugs and put a teabag in each.

Jennifer looked up in surprise and then laughed. "Oh, Ellen, you're so good for me! Scratch that last complaint. Forget I said it!" She held the teabag tabs as Ellen poured the steaming water. "But it is true that I don't know who the real Jennifer is.

"I don't even know what I look like . . . really. I see myself in the mirror, but only part of me. We never see ourselves as others do. I'm always surprised how I look in photographs."

Ellen nodded in agreement. "Yes, I often think, 'Is that what everyone has to look at?'"

"Exactly! Not that you're hard to look at," Jennifer laughed. "Oh, you know what I mean. But what do I look like? I don't really know. I know what my feet look like and I'd recognize my hands anywhere, and my kneecaps are quite ordinary, my arms and wrists. But I can't get out of myself to see everything. Even when I'm in front of a mirror, somehow I feel it's almost shameful to look long enough to get the whole picture. I look just enough to see straight, mousy hair that always sticks out in the wrong places, a nose that's skinny and too long, a narrow face, and a body that's skimpy in all the wrong places."

"Oh, Jennifer!" Ellen laughed and gave her a quick hug. "Now, let me tell you what I think you look like." She leaned back and surveyed her friend with a loving smile. "I see a very beautiful, open, friendly person in a well-maintained, efficient, and practical body with many attractive advantages: good health, shiny hair—not mousy at all—white, even teeth that turn a smile into a happening, strong legs that love to walk and run and play with children. Then there's inexpensive upkeep—you don't feel

45

obliged to spend hundreds of dollars on makeup and perfumes, and you aren't tempted so much by the packaging that you neglect the real Jennifer. But most of all, you're beautiful inside.

"Jennifer, don't be ashamed to look long at your mirror and take pride in who you are. God created you as a unique individual. And as for the person you are when you're with Corey or your students or me . . . you just react differently to different people, like we all do."

Jennifer sat absently twirling her empty cup in circles on the table, mulling over what Ellen had said. Ellen herself was a prime exhibit of her own words. She was prettier than Jennifer and had short, soft wavy hair that would have stayed just right if she were hanging upside down in a wind tunnel. But love and compassion outshone her appearance, and she was like a warm cookstove to a chilled and hungry soul. And others besides Jennifer came to her fires to warm themselves. *She probably does more good just talking with people who come into the store and with folks at church than I do teaching every day,* Jennifer thought.

The following Sunday night after the youth meeting while Corey was driving Jennifer home, she asked him the same question she had asked Ellen, explaining some of her feelings.

He listened carefully, then said, "Why do you think you're different in different situations? You always seem the same to me."

"That's just it. I am the same with you, but not with others."

"I've seen you with others, and you're the same."

"If you're around, maybe I am the same. Or maybe I just perceive myself differently."

"I'm the same all the time. I never change. I make it a practice not to change just as a matter of principle. I'm the same with you as with everyone else."

Jennifer grinned impishly. "Are you the same with other women as with me?"

He let the humor pass. "Yes, I am. I behave appropriately with all women and treat each with respect. And this business of looking in the mirror—I think you were right in thinking it a shameful thing. Well, perhaps not shameful, but certainly a waste of time. The Bible tells us that real beauty is not outward adorning but the inward cultivation of a gentle and quiet spirit. A man who has such a wife has a good, secure thing."

Jennifer frowned and wondered what he meant by that, but he went on. "And besides, it seems to me you were just fishing for some sort of compliment in that whole business!"

She couldn't see his face to tell whether he was serious or joking, but she decided she would interpret it as the latter. "Oh, absolutely! I can't survive on less than thirteen compliments a day, and since I get only eight or nine from you, I have to go fishing where it's most promising."

One of Corey's favorite topics for conversation was the husband-wife relationship. Every time he brought up the subject, Jennifer smiled inwardly, for although he had never actually proposed to her, he would talk very seriously about the duties and responsibilities of a pastor's wife.

A few days after her talk with Ellen, he raised the subject again. This time he focused on the Bible passages about submission, obedience, chastity, and a quiet and gentle spirit, as well as those touching on the husband's duty to keep his household and children in line.

"Don't you think, though," mused Jennifer, "that Ephesians puts some of the burden of change on the husband . . .

47

that it's not just the husband cracking the whip and the wife snapping to attention?"

He looked at her as though she were suggesting that Paul was a ticket salesman for the Roman circuses. "Of course it does! There's very heavy responsibility on husbands. Even as Christ makes the church holy and blameless, presenting her without stain or wrinkle, so husbands are to do the same thing. They are responsible for the spiritual well-being of their wives, and all these other things— submission, obedience, a quiet and gentle spirit— are a part of that."

"But what about 'Husbands, love your wives, as Christ loved the church'? Isn't that directed toward shaping the husband?"

"Absolutely. Love isn't just a feeling—it's *doing*, doing what is best for the beloved. A husband is obligated to love his wife by seeing to her spiritual welfare in all these matters. And he's responsible to love his children by giving them proper training and discipline. You're absolutely right! A husband and father has a weighty burden!"

They talked of other things, too—politics, creeping liberalism, moral laxity even in Christian circles, and the things being taught these days in the schools. Jennifer used that particular occasion to show him a poem by Christina Rossetti that Nola Mae had left on her desk. It spoke of ointment and virgins and cherubs and wheels, and Jennifer hoped Corey would be able to tell her what it meant and help her assess it. He read it through and said it was one of those things that has a biblical ring but is all the more dangerous in its obscurity. "You'd be well-advised to stick with Christian literature that has a plainer meaning," he said as he handed it back to her. His counsel seemed to confirm her own feeling, but she took the poem home and reread it several times, becoming more confused as the verse became more clear. It moved her spiritual emotions as nothing had done in a long time, so she decided to put it in a drawer and make her judgment later as to just how dangerous it was.

8   In the classroom, Jennifer began to develop a feel for each of her pupil's particular strengths and foibles. Selena and Olivia Reggis, for instance, were problems only when they had been sent to school without breakfast. And third-grader Joel Lindel, being young and immature, felt immensely overshadowed by his fourth-grade sister Cindy.

But Rosalie, with her peculiar absence of foibles despite her handicap, remained an enigma, and Jennifer felt a pressing curiosity about the influences that had shaped the child. Rosalie referred often to her father in terms of largeness, and to her mother she attributed beauty and gentleness. Just how had these simple farm folk earned such esteem in the child's eyes?

Had she owned a car, Jennifer might have visited the Baker farm early in the school year. But her only other means of getting there was a four-or-five-mile foot trail that wound through the hills, and after her last experience in the woods, she didn't relish the idea of going that way alone. So she procrastinated.

But after a particularly intriguing session of "finger talk" with Rosalie, Jennifer could endure her curiosity no longer, borrowed Corey's car, and set out on a crisp November Saturday.

She crossed the river at Plum and drove up the steep, winding road toward Plaggett Knob. Turning many tight corners, she passed precipitous driveways that either

49

ascended or descended at impossible angles to little plots of hillside stitched about with rail fences. Shabby houses and old log outbuildings grappled for whatever level ground there was, a reflection of the hardy, independent folk who fought for a living in this perpendicular land.

Just after she had passed a piney area that was being logged, Jennifer spotted the Baker mailbox and the long, steep driveway that marked the entrance to the farm. She bumped carefully up the rutted drive till she came to the open slopes of hard-won farmland.

The spread was small—house, barn, and assorted sheds. The remains of a garden, tomato vines still sagging on sticks and dried corn stalks tilting at odd angles, claimed kinship with the weather-beaten house. In a large pasture uphill from the buildings were a number of beef cattle, and beyond them, at the base of the woods, huddled a small, dilapidated sugarhouse.

Below the drive, a few sheep searched out a smaller, more closely cropped pasture for whatever grass they could find, and behind them the uneven buzz of a chainsaw emanated from the woodlot.

The place was run-down and poor but not unkempt. The farm implements were old but didn't have the look of abandonment like so many she had seen on the way up. And the wood near the back door had been split and carefully stacked.

Jennifer sat in the car for a long time, for when she tried to open the door, a brown and white lop-eared mongrel proved most unfriendly, growling and snarling with teeth bared. She drove as close to the house as she could, hoping Rosalie would see the car, and to her relief the child soon came running out. With a quick order to the dog, she freed Jennifer from her prison.

Rosalie was so overjoyed to see her teacher that she leaped into her arms with an exhuberant hug and then led her into the house.

Jennifer was surprised at how neat and clean everything looked and complimented Rosalie on it. For a girl of ten, she displayed considerable domestic aptitude. But Rosalie's delight was her room and her dolls, which she showed Jennifer with pride. Her doll collection was unique, for the child had made them all herself from such materials as balled grass and leaves, corn husks, a lightbulb, scraps of fabric, and carefully carved wood. Jennifer had seen her deftly making dolls at school, but had had no idea of the breadth of her creative ability.

Before they left her room, Rosalie picked up one doll, then another, and finally decided on a different one still and presented it to Jennifer. "For you," she signed, "I love you!" Tears came to Jennifer's eyes as she hugged the child and replied, "Thank you. You are special. The doll is special because you made it and gave it to me."

Then Rosalie led Jennifer outside to meet her "friends." First, she introduced her to Mouse, her intrepid canine guardian. Jennifer was surprised at so unlikely a name, but learned that a friend of Mr. Baker's had given Rosalie the pup with a name that he said would fool intruders— whereupon Mouse would eat them up! The dog looked civil enough now, but Jennifer didn't trust her hand to him and just spoke politely instead.

Next, they went to the barn and climbed up into the haymow where three lively kittens tumbled about. Jennifer was slow to understand the signs Rosalie used for their names. She would make an *e* and then point to her knee, then point to herself, and again to her knee, and once again point to herself and then to her knee: Eeny, Meeny, and Miny. When Jennifer had comprehended that much, Rosalie signed in all seriousness, "No more."

Jennifer laughed aloud, but seeing that the aural pun was lost on Rosalie, she asked, "Who told you there was no more? Your father?"

51

"No. Justin, Father's friend."

"Did he name the kittens, too?"

Rosalie nodded.

"Never mind," Jennifer chuckled, "maybe there will be more someday. Why don't you name your very next kitten More and then tell Justin. He'll probably laugh, too!"

Just then Jennifer heard the clank of chains coming out of the woods. A black horse in logging harness with the driver standing on the rigging was coming up a narrow lane toward the barn. Rosalie ran to greet her father and gave the horse, Tom, a pat on his steaming neck. Jennifer walked over to meet Mr. Baker, surprised that the "largeness" attributed to him by Rosalie was other than stature.

Orley Baker, a small, spare man in his mid-fifties, bore a marked resemblance to the impoverished pasture, the woebegone house, the dusty, barren yard; he was part and parcel of this forlorn, unproductive farm, and his face showed evidence of long acquaintance with hardship. But his crinkled eyes and smile were those of a man who had known joy and laughter along with sorrow. He seemed genuinely glad to meet "Miz Darrow," and after he had taken care of Tom, he invited Jennifer into the house again for a cup of coffee.

The opportunity to talk with Orley Baker gave Jennifer a new perspective on Rosalie's special personality, her needs and problems. Though Orley lacked some material goods, he lavished love on his daughter. And because of the vicissitudes of life on this farm, Rosalie had none of the laziness and self-indulgence that Jennifer saw in some children.

Orley liked to talk, especially about his troubles. His father had been a miner, and he himself had worked in the mines until he was in his thirties. But after two accidents—first, being trapped four days in a cave-in, and then an explosion which left him deathly afraid of fire—he quit and took over the farm of a brother who had been killed when a tractor rolled over on him.

Then he married Sara who had brought a special dimension to his life. "Wa'n't much of a looker, but she had a warm heart," he said gruffly, covering his emotion. Rosalie was born when Orley was forty-two and Sara thirty-four. Rosalie contracted scarlet fever when she was three, and the high fever left her deaf, a severe blow to both parents. But Sara, with an urgency Orley thought was a "premonition," learned sign language and worked single-mindedly at teaching both Rosalie and Orley. When Rosalie was six, Sara developed a fast and virulent form of cancer and suffered a painful death. "That was onct I was thankful the child couldn't hear," he said directly to Jennifer while Rosalie was out of the room. She came back a minute later with a picture of her mother. Sara indeed wasn't a "good looker"—Rosalie's delicate features came from her father— but seeing the look of kindness and compassion in the face of this courageous woman, Jennifer knew that Rosalie had received a rich heritage from her mother. Jennifer wished she had known the woman.

Jennifer asked Orley if he managed the farm by himself. He said he mostly did, with a little help now and again from his friend Justin. It was hard, he said, and he did a little of this and that to put a few dollars in his pocket. Right now he was logging out some of his pine. Normally softwoods of any kind were unsaleable, at least locally, because the mills were set up for hardwood and didn't want to bother with what little pine and hemlock there was. But "a feller downstate wantin' t' build one o' them fancy lodges" had offered him a pretty good price for three thousand board feet of logs on the roadside, so Orley, with only momentary regret, cut into his stand to meet the request.

In the spring he would make some maple syrup. Not

much o' that in these parts, neither. Folks as tasted th' syrup they make up no'th say this don't hold a candle to it fer flavor, but still it brings in a few extry dollars." He raised a few head of cattle and some sheep and pigs and grew enough produce to keep the larder stocked all year. "Did hev some goats, but they all took sick an' died last spring."

This got Orley started on a whole history of disasters in recent years. He was truly born to trouble. One of his two milk cows had died last winter. A year ago he had broken his arm just at slaughtering time. His garden had suffered considerable hail damage. And varmints persisted in decimating his chicken flock, right under Mouse's supposedly watchful eye.

"He ain't good fer much 'cept'n t' keep a watch on Rosalie, but he's wuth his keep an' then some on that score. He don't 'low *nobody* near her 'cept by her leave . . . you noticed that, eh?" He chuckled as Jennifer nodded vigorously. "She bein' deaf an' all, hit's a comfort havin' th' dog t' look out fer her."

Orley gave a big sigh and rubbed his head. "With so much trouble as is already come about, y' jes' wonder when th' next crack o' lightnin's gonna hit . . . 'r where, fer that matter. Gittin' nuf money t' live on is allus a worry, but not th' biggest one. Rosalie an' me ain't got much, but we allus got food on th' table and a roof over our heads. But sumpin's allus goin' wrong with one o' th' machines, an' they ain't easy t' git fixed.

"An' then I worry 'bout Rosalie, what she'd come to if anythin' happened t' me. She's a good girl an' able t' do a lot, but she is deaf, an' that ain't easy in this world."

"Surely someone would take care of her," Jennifer replied. "Do you have any family anywhere, or your friend— wouldn't he take her in?"

"No, I ain't got nobody left. An' Justin, he don't like t' talk about them things like I do. He gits mad when I worry an' says I shouldn't be even thinkin' 'bout sech things happenin' . . . that's what makes 'em come about, he says."

Jennifer's heart was heavy as she drove home, full of the weight of sorrow and anxiety borne by this little man who worked so hard just to keep himself and his daughter alive. But it was also full of love for the child who was such a bright spot in her own life as well as Orley's. She had thoroughly enjoyed the visit—the tour of the place with Rosalie and the long talk over coffee with her father. They had both expressed enthusiastically their appreciation for her visit.

Jennifer wondered what Corey would think of her visit. Most likely he would ask her what she had said and if she had moved the conversation to the Bakers' need for Jesus. Well, they'd talked about need, all right, but probably not the right kind, according to Corey.

She looked down. On the seat beside her was the little doll Rosalie had given her. Exquisitely made from multicolored and multitextured broom straws that must have taken ages to collect, it seemed almost the essence of Rosalie herself. A pale-yellow apron and matching bonnet set off the delicate green blouse with its short flounce over the broom skirt.

Tears came to Jennifer's eyes. "Oh, Rosalie, you who have so little gave me so much today!"

9   On the Friday before Election Day, Nola Mae came home late in the afternoon. If a wrong-number phone call hadn't pulled Jennifer out of the

bedroom where she had been changing sheets, she might have missed the pyrotechnics altogether. Nola Mae, red-faced and angry almost to the point of tears, banged down her school things and wouldn't say anything but "Oh, just shut up!" in answer to Jennifer's questions. She steamed on into her bedroom, slamming the door as hard as she could, and stayed there for about an hour.

Having never seen her in such a state, Jennifer was a trifle concerned, but Nola Mae finally emerged, much the same as always. They ate in perhaps a little deeper silence than normal, but afterward Nola Mae went off as usual to visit friends "in the real world," as she called it.

The next day Jennifer found out what had happened. She had known about the electioneering scheduled for Friday afternoon but had chosen instead to go home and catch up on some housework. It was to be quite a big affair for Clevis. The handsome young candidate for U. S. Senate was swinging by town, and the town, in response, was making elaborate preparation. The lawn in front of the library had sprouted a loudspeaker-equipped platform generously festooned with red, white, and blue bunting. Flags fluttered elsewhere, especially in front of the establishments of his conservative supporters. Across Hubert Smith's store front a large sign boomed, "WELCOME TO OUR NEXT U S SENATER." Folks all over town looked forward to the event, and the promise of the Firemen's Auxiliary to donate their Friday bake-sale items for refreshments didn't hurt the cause any.

So even though Jennifer had not taken in the politicking, she went to the Post Office the next day eager to talk with someone who could fill her in on the occasion. Ellen Lindel was chatting at the window with the postmistress, Frieda Copp, a rather formidable no-nonsense person built along the lines of a tank. She was what Kenny Stuckworth termed

56

"one o' them grain-fed wimmin," but she had a good heart and knew just about everything that went on in town.

Jennifer asked how the speechifying had gone, remarking on Nola Mae's strange behavior. "She was fit to be tied when she came in and wouldn't say anything! Do you know what happened?"

Both of the other women began to laugh and pieced together for Jennifer the events of the previous afternoon.

The senatorial hopeful had arrived in his limousine and made his way to the crowd on the library lawn amid much milling and jockeying for position. Miss Sadie was the most tenacious, however, and bent his ear with all the good things about Clevis she could think of, even mentioning Jennifer's sign language skill and work with young people. The candidate tried to listen as best he could while shaking hands and smiling and patting small heads.

Just before he was to mount the platform, Nola Mae was introduced to him as "one of our fine public school teachers." This gave him an inspiration which he put into action by pulling the girl up onto the platform with him. Firmly holding her hand, he extolled her as a fine example of individual achievement without government handouts. Here was a young lady, he said, a lover of common folk who used her talents to help the deaf, the poor and disadvantaged, and who devoted much time and energy to working with the youth of the area. On and on he went, embroidering on what he remembered of Miss Sadie's comments about Jennifer.

Most of the townsfolk were smiling broadly, if not snickering, over the mixup, but Wesley Bishop, who had visited Tully's Lounge before coming across the street, cheered and clapped in loud agreement, to Nola Mae's intense mortification. Not till the would-be senator had launched into his diatribe against "bleeding-heart liberals" was she able to escape, and she fled the scene with the red face with which she had entered the house, Wesley's cries of "Atta girl, Nola Mae!" following her.

With just a touch of malicious satisfaction, Jennifer laughed till the tears rolled as the women concluded their story, but she resolved to say nothing further about the incident to her beleaguered housemate.

She then started out the door but turned back to ask if anyone had seen Tikki Granger in the past two weeks.

"Tully was talkin' about him just yesterday," replied Frieda. "Said he hadn't seen him around for a spell. He ain't been botherin' you agin, has he?"

"Oh, no. I was just wondering."

Jennifer herself saw him the following week during afternoon recess. He came striding along one of the several paths that crisscrossed the schoolyard, and with a fair amount of trepidation she went over to speak to him, anticipating some sign of transformation. But nothing except hostility showed in his eyes, and with a couple of venomous words, he brushed past her and went on toward town.

She stood looking after him in some confusion. He might have shown just a little friendliness in the wake of his mishap, but evidently it wasn't to be. With a shake of her head, she turned back just as Rosalie ran up and grabbed her hand, pointing with anguish in her face at the broad back disappearing among the trees. Jennifer held her close for a moment, anger rising inside. Who had been frightening the child with tales of Tikki Granger? The Reggis girls perhaps?

To distract Rosalie, she took her inside to get a poem Nola Mae had set out just that morning. Jennifer had liked it right away and had put it with her school things to show to Rosalie.

Little Lamb, who made thee?
Dost thou know who made thee?
Gave thee life, and bade thee feed,
By the stream and o'er the mead;
Gave thee clothing of delight,
Softest clothing, woolly, bright;
Gave thee such a tender voice,
Making all the vales rejoice?
Little Lamb, who made thee?
Dost thou know who made thee?

Little Lamb, I'll tell thee,
Little Lamb, I'll tell thee:
He is callèd by thy name,
For He calls Himself a Lamb,
He is meek, and He is mild;
He became a little child.
I a child, and thou a lamb,
We are callèd by His name.
Little Lamb, God bless thee!
Little Lamb, God bless thee!

That evening, Jennifer decided to share with Nola Mae how much Rosalie had enjoyed the poem and how together they had worked it out in sign language. She thought she might even have Rosalie do it for the whole class sometime. "I really appreciate your giving it to me. I liked it very much."

But Nola Mae just huffed at her. "You use one lousy little poem out of all I've given you. What about the rest of them? They're good, too!"

Jennifer bit her lip. "Maybe they are, but I just don't understand them."

"You might try reading them a few times. They're not like your silly doggerel that wears thin the first time through. And it's the same with your music—nothing but fluff. It might interest you to know," she added superciliously, "that some of the greatest art, music, and literature has come out of the Christian tradition, but you don't know a thing about any of it!"

Jennifer got up and walked away, fighting back tears. Sick and tired of Nola Mae and her books and music, tired of always being the view at the end of Nola Mae's nose, she wished Nola Mae would go out so she could wallow in her "fluff" with the volume turned up full blast.

She got some comfort and help from Ellen in her effort to remain sweet and unflappable in the face of Nola Mae's sharp tongue. She also received encouragement to read whatever Nola Mae gave her and to try to be as positive as she could about it.

"After all," Ellen mused, "it's quite remarkable that it's Christian poetry she's trying to get you to read!"

"But Corey says—"

"Corey is a minister, and a fine one—not a student of literature. Nola Mae is the expert there."

Jennifer had never thought of Nola Mae as an expert at anything except a put-down. She found it hard to look at her in that role and to swallow her pride enough to accept tutelage from her in things Christian. But some of those poems did have a lot more to them than she first thought.

But we from south and north,
From east and west, a feeble folk who came
By desert ways in quest of land unseen,
A promised land of pasture ever green
And ever springing ever singing wave,
Know best Thy Name of Jesus: Blessed Name,
Man's life and resurrection from the grave.

She dug out the folder she had stuffed them in and began reading.

10 "Oh, Ellen," wailed Jennifer over the phone, "I'm in a terrible fix! Corey just phoned. His folks are due this morning, and he just got a call from someone in Plum whose son is threatening suicide. He asked if I'd please meet his folks at the church and then give them some lunch!"

"Oh, my!"

"Exactly! I don't know what to do! I'm scared to death to meet them alone. I was counting on Corey being there. And I don't know what to do about lunch. I can't bring them here—" she lowered her voice. "Nola Mae has stuff spread all over the place, getting ready to leave for Thanksgiving vacation. Even if they were the kind who could handle a little mess, I still wouldn't want to inflict Nola Mae on them right off."

"Or vice versa."

"Well, yes—maybe. Ellen, do you suppose if I brought over some food, I could use a very small corner of—"

"Stop right there. You go to the church and meet them. I can't help you with that. What time are they coming?"

"Somewhere between ten and eleven."

"All right. You meet them and bring them here, and I'll have lunch ready around noon. It won't be fancy, but it'll be better than Cooper's luncheonette. Rosalie is here for the weekend with Cindy, so I'll be fixing something a little special anyway. She'll be glad to have you here for lunch."

Jennifer hung up the receiver with a sense of relief, but also foreboding. She hadn't expected to have to face Corey's parents till evening, and in his company. She now had less than an hour to compose herself and get to the church. What was it Nola Mae had quoted a while back? Something about knowing you're to be hanged in a fortnight wonderfully concentrates the mind. Well, she had better start concentrating.

She reached the church just before ten and willed for

61

them to get hopelessly lost and not arrive till noon. But at 10:25 they were there. Fixing on her most friendly smile, she went out into the gray November air to greet the couple climbing out of their sleek gray Oldsmobile.

Jennifer had been giving herself encouraging speeches that once they were here it would be all right, and that their friendliness would eliminate her own unease. But it wasn't and they weren't. Though polite and cordial enough, a stiff formality smothered any incipient friendliness that might have been lurking in them. For one thing, Corey's absence gave them no little annoyance. Perhaps they, too, had wanted a buffer period to prepare themselves for meeting Jennifer.

Jennifer was decidedly uncomfortable. She thought she had dressed carefully, but relative to the elegance before her, even Nola Mae would have looked frumpy. After they had chatted about the cold, raw weather, the probability of rain, and how their trip had been, there seemed to be absolutely nothing else to say. Finally, Mr. Witham cleared his throat and suggested they have a look round the church. So Jennifer conducted them—very slowly—through every nook and cranny of the building, painstakingly pulling from her memory all the crumbs of historical information she knew about Clevis Baptist Church.

When she had exhausted that resource, she looked hopefully at her watch—only 11:15. If they had seemed the walking sort and if the day had been nicer, she might have strolled them through town, but Jennifer thought it wise to drive instead. She hoped they might want to see the parsonage right away. That would kill the better part of a half hour just driving to Dorsil and back, but they wanted to wait till Corey was with them. Finally, in desperation Jennifer led them to Ellen's, hoping her friend would forgive her for bringing them early.

Ellen greeted them all warmly and graciously, and a

wave of gratitude came over Jennifer for this haven of friendship. Rosalie bounded into the kitchen with a big hug for her teacher and friend and began a rapid recitation of events in her visit with Cindy. Jennifer directed her attention to the two people she had failed to notice in her excitement.

Jennifer signed, "Rosalie, I would like you to meet Mr. and Mrs. Witham—Pastor Witham's mother and father."

Rosalie gaped at such unaccustomed magnificence, then extended her hand in greeting. Mrs. Witham barely touched it with her gloved hand, but Mr. Witham shook it firmly with a loud, "How do you do, Rosalie?"

"This must be the child Corey told us about who is—ah—hard of hearing?" he said.

"Yes, Rosalie is deaf," Jennifer replied.

"How very sad. Nothing can be done about it?"

Jennifer turned Rosalie, who was still staring at the Withams, toward Cindy, who had followed her friend to the kitchen but was keeping out of introduction range. "Go play for a while longer. Lunch will be ready soon."

Now that they had hit on a topic of conversation about which she was knowledgeable, Jennifer checked first with Ellen to make sure she didn't need help in the kitchen, then led Corey's parents into the living room and hung their coats in the closet. Then she talked at length about Rosalie and her special gifts and about her own involvement as Rosalie's teacher.

Lunch was tasteful and beautifully served. "After one look at them," Ellen whispered to Jennifer, "I put away the chipped stoneware and got out the china!" The conversation went quite smoothly, with Ellen's help, but Jennifer was surprised and a bit chagrined by Rosalie's wriggling, signing, and strange noises during the meal. In the presence of these two austere, coldly mannered visitors, it seemed . . . repulsive—even ugly. Jennifer reminded herself harshly, *Rosalie is not ugly* and was disgusted with herself for even thinking it.

The Withams talked a bit with the Lindel children but were obviously uncomfortable around Rosalie. She sensed this and was not particularly endearing either during the meal or afterward as they all sat in the living room.

With the arrival of Corey, who had found Jennifer's note at the church, spirits lifted. Parents and son exchanged greetings, and the Withams thanked Ellen graciously for her hospitality. They went to each of the children in turn, but when they got to Rosalie, she was leaning back in her chair, eyes shut.

"Oh, she's sleeping, poor child. Don't disturb her." But Jennifer wanted to shake her in exasperation. If anyone else had been aware of the insult implicit in her closed eyes, Jennifer would have removed her from the room and talked with her—very seriously, but as it went unnoticed, she thought it prudent to drop the matter, at least for now.

On the way out, Jennifer gave Ellen a grateful hug. "Just name your price," she whispered. "I'll baby-sit, scrub floors, clean the cellar, anything in return for what you've done today!"

"I'll keep it in mind," Ellen smiled and squeezed her friend's hand.

As the week progressed and Jennifer saw more of the Withams, she still was not at ease with them. They did become more cordial toward her—indeed, hardly less cordial than they were to Corey. She was expecting them to dote on their only son, but they seemed rather critical of him, as if to keep him at arm's length. Perfection seemed their standard—at least in the front they presented to the world. And such a front! Never a hair out of place, never a wrong move.

Jennifer saw clearly the ways they had molded and shaped Corey into their own image: his fastidiousness and concern about appearances, his pride, his difficulty in being at ease and relaxed with people. But they had also helped forge his strengths: self-confidence; the ability to work long and hard and to make things happen; a knack for cutting through peripheral matters to get to the essence of an issue, whether at a deacons' meeting or in formulating a five-year plan for the church. There were differences, of course. Corey showed more patience than his parents toward the failures of others, and he was more realistic than they about how high to set his standards. At any rate, Jennifer came to know Corey in a deeper way through getting acquainted with his parents, and after a few days she was less in awe of them, though she couldn't get over the feeling that there would never be anyone quite good enough to be Corey's wife.

Thanksgiving Day dawned bright and clear, though colder even than the earlier part of the week. The rains had moved off, leaving ice-trimmed puddles in valley areas and snow on the higher elevations.

Football teams everywhere were preparing for the final tilt of the season, coming forth in the full splendor of their panoply with retinue of cheerleaders and marching bands. "Indeed," Nola Mae frequently huffed, "in every school system music and art are the poor relation to football, and the only reason music gets any money at all is that the band is necessary to all that macho pomposity!"

The day was both good and bad, depending on whom you talked to. Jensen lost to their arch rival, Cranmere, because their star quarterback had been injured in the previous week's game, and the replacement, so nervous he threw up three times before the game, caused two costly fumbles during the first quarter.

If photographs could have been taken around Clevis and

Dorsil to capture the essence of different celebrations, the good and the bad would have stood out in sharp relief.

Nola Mae would be posed near the ski lodge fireplace, drink in hand, eyes sparkling with wit and repartee, surrounded by admirers, fully alive in her natural habitat.

On Hazel Lane, the Potters with their visiting family would be caught watching football in their bright, cheerful sitting room. Mrs. Potter, tired from worrying over the festal preparation her daughter had made, would be saying, "I declare, this time o' year is so busy. I can't keep up with it all. You people here today, and I suppose we'll be at your place for Christmas. Seems like it's been one thing after another we bin gaddin' off to all fall. September we had a doctor's appointment, and then in October—Ed, didn't we go someplace?—oh, I know! 'Twas Annie Murphy's birthday we was invited to, on October 11. She was ninety and still spry as a teakettle. Why, her son Henry is a sight worse off 'n she is. But I reckon if Annie kin stand up t' bury two husbands, she kin bury a son, too."

The evening scene at the parsonage in Dorsil would also have reflected tranquility. It had been a good day with an excellent meal in Jensen, and now an affable warmth rested upon the foursome. The camera would have caught the pleased glow on Jennifer's face as Mr. Witham took her hand in commendation of her stand with him against the other two in a discussion on environmental concerns.

The essence of the Lindel's Thanksgiving would have shown up most graphically at bedtime. Ellen lay cold and resentful, unresponsive to Randy's frustrated attempts at pacification. "If I'd known you'd go into such a bark, I'd have eaten the whole bowl of stuffing! Why do you let things like that bother you so long?"

It had been a long, tiring day, and Ellen had to fight to keep her voice steady. "I made the mistake of telling you it was a new recipe, and you wouldn't even touch it."

"I did take some, and I didn't like it."

"Only because it was different. If you didn't have the old to compare it with, you'd have liked it fine. Everything doesn't have to taste the same, you know. I spent an hour and a half making it as a special offering of love. How do you think I feel?"

"What else can I do but say I'm sorry? But that isn't enough for you. Do you want me to go out now and eat the rest of it?"

"I work so hard getting the kids to eat things they don't particularly like, and then you destroy it all in a minute by—"

"Oh, come on, Ellen, this is utterly stupid. It isn't worth going on and on about. Give me a kiss and we'll laugh about it in the morning."

She lay there in the darkness, tears rolling down into her hair, pulled from opposite sides by love and injury. But she turned away, stiff and hurt, a shapeless blob of turkey dressing between them.

There was one other transaction that day, but the camera would have caught only two pairs of hands reaching out of the darkness behind the church, one placing a large box into the hands of the other, then both parties melting back into the darkness.

Sunday, the last day the senior Withams were around, continued clear and cold. Jennifer thought the two might stay in Dorsil for the eleven o'clock service there, but they drove up with Corey a little after nine and chatted with Jennifer as she made preparations for her Sunday school class.

The sanctuary looked particularly nice this bright, crisp morning, with colorful bouquets on the piano, on the communion table, and on a low cloth-covered table.

"Did Corey have a funeral this week, that we should receive such bounty?" Ellen inquired of Jennifer.

"Not that I know of, and anyway, they're too pretty for funeral arrangements."

Ellen gave hearty agreement. "When I die, give me daisies or dandelions. Anything but gladiolas!"

The service was characteristic of Corey, with a lofty passage that led into his favorite judgment motif. But less than five minutes into the message, a restlessness began among those in the front which quickly turned to outright panic and hysteria. It spread from front to back, and soon the entire church was in an uproar, with almost all the women and children and not a few men up on the pews. At first, Jennifer could not determine what was happening. Then she heard the word, "snakes," and saw them emerging from the draped flower stand. They were sluggish, evidently having been brought in from the cold to warm up during the service, and some, still tangled together, were being dragged along by the more lively ones.

With the same sort of involuntary shudder that was passing through the rest of the terror-stricken group, Jennifer looked up at Corey to see what he would say or do, but for once he was at a loss and stood staring in disbelief. Then some of the less fearful men began hollering for brooms and containers for collecting the reptiles.

By this time Corey had begun to call for calm—from the safety of the platform. But it was his mother who most effectively settled things down. As soon as she had grasped the situation, she pushed past her husband and Jennifer and stepped into the aisle. Striding purposefully toward the largest and most fearsome of the snakes, she unhesitatingly placed her trim, pale blue sandal squarely on its head and neck to hold it until the cleanup crew got itself organized.

"That was a water snake, too," Randy said afterward,

"and they can be pretty nasty. "I don't know what kept it from striking at her. But then, I guess we should be thankful that Granger and Company didn't send us any rattlers or copperheads!"

Church was over. There was no salvaging the service, even after ridding the sanctuary of the remaining snakes, some two dozen or more altogether. But Jennifer never forgot Mrs. Witham's defiant, triumphant look of total self-control as she took her indomitable stand on a platform no one else cared to share.

11 Jennifer came back tired from the Christmas holidays. She had left for her parents' home near Philadelphia with hopes of sleeping late every day and going to bed early, but it was not to be. Parties and family activities kept her constantly on the go. Then, because she was rundown physically, she caught a cold. So she dragged herself to Clevis after an all-too-short vacation, glad, however, to be back, at least for Corey's sake.

The several letters and phone calls she had received from him bore eloquent witness to his loneliness. Her first night back, they went out to eat. But later, too tired even to sleep, Jennifer lay in bed reflecting on the evening. She had been anxious to see Corey and tell him all about her holiday, but with a sense of disquietude she realized that she hadn't been able to be honest with him. For example, her sister had taken her to see an excellent new film. But Corey disapproved of movies, so she just hadn't bothered to tell him about it.

As she lay there struggling with her feelings about Corey and their relationship, another aspect of her return hit full force. On Thursday evening she would begin teaching an adult remedial reading class that would meet weekly. She hadn't wanted to take on anything additional, but the school board had pleaded with her and Corey had encouraged her to do it. Reluctantly, she agreed. To teach children was one thing, to teach adults quite another. Furthermore, she wasn't prepared. She had been determined not to spoil her vacation with too much homework, but now with the class only five days away, nothing was ready.

She suddenly felt stifled. Slipping on her warmest robe, she tiptoed out to the side porch and stood in the crisp stillness, looking up at the stars. With the shock of icy air entering her lungs, the stars seemed to dance and skip in some celestial celebration. The river, which sometimes seemed so muffled, now sounded as near as the foot of the driveway.

> Waters ripple and flow,
>   Slowly passes each day,
> Faithless lover of mine,
>   Stay no longer away . . .

"Faithless lover . . . " Corey faithless? Never! No, if anything, she felt hemmed in by his solicitude, his carefully programmed management of her life.

But Corey was not the only problem. She was losing control of things at school, too. She didn't want to teach that class, but getting out of it now seemed impossible. Why was she dreading it so much? The group would be small, mostly people she was at least acquainted with. Ruth and Ed Carlish from church, hoping to be able to read the Bible more easily; Galina Kostyukov, seeking to improve her sketchy English; Jim Baker, a farmer who had never learned to read; and Kinney Previn, a high-school girl. She had no cause for concern over those five. But still

70

she shivered, and not altogether from the cold.

She took one last look at the stars, by now solid and steady, moving through their courses with an unwavering stability that reached far beyond the infinitesimal perimeters of her problems.

At 7:15 on Thursday evening, Jennifer was in Nola Mae's classroom, since the scaled-down desks in her own room were too small for adults. Some of her nervousness was beginning to drain away, as the five who had signed up for the class were eager to learn. Ruth and Ed and Kinney read fairly well, but Galina and Jim were back at square one. Such a small class, however, would give opportunity for individual attention.

But disaster struck at 7:18 in the form of Tikki, Kenny Stuckworth, and Joey Hamlin. Grinning foolishly and snickering among themselves, they slouched in and lined themselves in front of the desk.

Jennifer's heart froze. Just the thought of these men in the class frightened her, and she was sure they were there to cause trouble. For a brief moment she felt like getting up and running out the door.

Needing to make a decision within fifteen seconds, she straightened her shoulders and sized them up. Of the three, Kenny appeared the least likely to inspire anything in anybody. Big and gangly, like an off-duty marionette, he walked with a slight limp from a mine accident. Joey was compactly built, with a pugnaciousness that more than compensated for his small size. They all looked seedy and unshaven, but they were reasonably clean—and not drunk! Jennifer wasn't sure if their sobriety was good or bad, however: had they come in smelling of liquor, she would have been justified in sending them packing. As it was, she could think of no real reason, other than her gut feeling, to bar them from the class.

She looked straight at Tikki, knowing him to be com-

71

mander of the escapade. "If you are here to learn," she said sternly, "you're welcome to join the class. But if you just want to make trouble—"

"Oh, no, ma'am. They won't be no trouble from us. Me'n th' boys'll be real good. We'll jes' set down over here, an' you go right ahead with yer lesson." He took a seat behind Galina, and the other two sat on either side of him.

With considerable misgiving, Jennifer tried to pull together her shattered plans. She had intended to play some simple word games to put everyone at ease that first night, but now she wasn't sure just how to proceed. Outwardly, the three were behaving quite well, discounting some sniggering and whispering, but the psychological stress twisted every nerve within her.

To give herself more time to think, she picked up where she had left off in trying to determine the reading level of each person. Handing books to the trio for them to read aloud, she soon found, to her surprise, that Kenny and Joey read quite well. Tikki, also to her surprise, read poorly. Somehow, perhaps because of his reputation, she had expected him to be able to read better than anyone in the group, but he struggled along at a third grade level.

About halfway through the session, Tikki, leaning forward and apparently listening intently, began muttering under his breath, whereupon Galina sat up with a startled look on her face. The look grew more and more pained until she burst out crying and headed for the door.

Astonished, Jennifer jumped up and got to her before she went out. "What happened, Galina? What made you cry? Was it something I said that you didn't understand?"

The Russian woman shook her head violently. "It wass him," pointing to Tikki. "He keep saying tings, bad tings—in Russian!"

"Russian! How could he be saying things in Russian?"

"I don't know. He call me bad names."

Jennifer turned back toward Tikki, but he had already moved to another seat, far away from Galina's chair. So with assurances that it wouldn't happen again, Galina returned to her place, and the evening drew to an uneasy conclusion.

The following two weeks, the class went much the same. Tikki, Joey, and Kenny came on time and made some effort to learn, but they were vulgar, rude, and always on the verge of causing trouble. They managed, however, to avoid being asked to leave by virtue of the strict control Tikki exercised over the other two. With some uncanny instinct he knew exactly when to draw the rein and played Jennifer's nerves like a skilled musician.

As January ran down, so did Jennifer. Tired and discouraged, she even resented Corey and his boundless energy. But she attributed it to mid-winter blues and forced herself to keep up with her lesson plans, youth work, and Thursday night reading class.

12 Miss Sadie McCusker was rather out of sorts that winter. Normally she was easy enough to get along with, provided you allowed for her patrician ways and somewhat ascerbic tongue. But at this particular time, circumstances seemed to conspire to bring down her exterior gentility.

It had all started during the general gift distribution at the church Christmas party when she received a beautifully wrapped but anonymous gift. She was surprised and flattered as she unwrapped it, carefully keeping the paper intact and saving the bow. A T-shirt came forth, folded backward, so that when she held it up everyone but she could see what was on the front. At the ensuing laughter, she turned it around and read to her mortification, "Tully's Lounge—Put a Barrel In Your Chest." With head high and lips tightly compressed, she gathered it up, neatly folded paper, bow, and all, and primly deposited it in the wastebasket standing by the refreshment table. Her social intercourse cooled notably after that.

Then, too, Corey brought her no little annoyance with his changes in the order of worship starting the first Sunday in January. No one could remember the order ever being tampered with, and she spent considerable time trying to get him to see reason. She was not the oldest living member, she told him—Granny Scopps over in the Jensen Nursing Home had joined the church three years earlier than she— but she was the oldest *active* member, and that ought to count for something. But he was adamant and she was miffed. It seemed somehow a desecration of a holy thing, and she made sure everyone knew of her displeasure.

The week after New Year's, a third thing came about, a bizarre accident involving her prize azalea near the corner of Main and Maple.

A freezing rain had left all the roads glare ice, none except Main Street having been salted. The church trustees had asked Bill Previn to give them an estimate on taking down a dead elm in the cemetery, and as it was too slippery that day to do any logging or hauling, he decided to drive by to look it over. He couldn't get up Maple Avenue and so drove around by way of Elm Street, parking his pickup near the top of the hill by the cemetery.

He had just gotten through the gate when he saw the truck begin to slide ever so slowly down the hill like a stately ocean liner moving out to sea. He shouted and started after it and promptly fell down. The vehicle gradually picked up speed as Bill slipped and swore and bellowed in its wake.

Meanwhile at the bottom of the hill, Ellen Lindel drove cautiously around the corner toward Miss Sadie's driveway. She was well onto Maple Avenue before she saw the driverless juggernaut drifting inexorably toward her. In total panic, she aimed for "Reverse," slammed instead into "Park," and sat immobile, engine revving wildly.

By this time the truck was almost upon her and beginning to yaw; she at last got into gear, but spun around, and the two vehicles touched sides gently and proceeded apace into Miss Sadie's azalea.

No one was hurt—fortunately for Miss Sadie. If there had been, she would have regretted her sharp salvo fired from the firm footing of her front porch.

Even Jennifer fell into disfavor and received a stern lecture on the need for better control of the youth group. After the first sizeable snowfall, the kids were all outside the church doing what kids from time immemorial have always done— even as far back as Miss Sadie's youth—throwing snowballs. The particular ball under consideration was lobbed at a long angle toward a spot on Main Street where no cars were at the moment. But the thrower did not allow for the physics of moving objects, one of which was Miss Sadie, driving toward home with her window cracked for health reasons. The trajectories of the two objects came together at a precise moment, and Miss Sadie had to stop to wipe her glasses.

And so Miss Sadie was in fine fettle on the last Thursday of the month when Joey Hamlin ran athwart her prow.

Joey was a slob, normally not caring what he looked like, hardly even washing at the end of his mine shift. But his small, muscular build pleased him well, and he liked to dress up occasionally to show it off to best effect. He had decided this particular Thursday evening to so dress for Jennifer's benefit. Though not a beauty, she was not unpleasant to look at, and Joey wanted to give the preacher a little competition.

75

Joey's taste in clothing ran to the loud end of things, and in addition he had a large gaudy ring of which he was inordinately proud and for which he had paid what was for him a large sum of money. Thus, 6:30 found him clean, shaven, and decked out in his best finery, buying cigarettes in Smith's Store.

On the way out, however, he skidded on a pencil someone had dropped and sprawled awkwardly through the doorway, giving his head a nasty rap on the door frame and nearly knocking Miss Sadie down the steps.

A number of people were in the store at the time, and hearing the racket, they came to the doorway in time to hear Miss Sadie give out her opinion of Joey Hamlin. Having been pre-heated by her other misfortunes, she lit into him, calling him a drunken bantam rooster and committing the unpardonable sin of laughing at his clothes and his beautiful ring. Having delivered herself of all this before he even had time to swear, she looked down her aristocratic nose and marched on through the laughing crowd into the store.

By the time Tikki, Joey, and Kenny got to class—late—all three were surly and grim. They had been arguing loudly in the hallway, and from what the other class members could hear, Tikki had taken strong exception to Joey's getting spruced up to impress the teacher. Joey was very angry, and just outside the door Tikki threatened to bash his head against the wall if he didn't simmer down. Evidently Joey had had sufficient experience with Tikki to take him at his word. However, the sullen undercurrent was like a volcano ready to blow.

Then, about a half-hour before the end of class, two huge men, both of them drunk, barged in demanding to see Tikki. Tikki was on his feet in an instant, but not before giving Jennifer a quick hand sign to end the class. The terrified students huddled in the front corner of the classroom as knives flashed on all sides.

Kinney moved close to Jennifer. "I think I kin slip out this door an' git Ray."

Jennifer, her face white and heart pounding, nodded. "Be careful!" she whispered.

But as Kinney disappeared through the door, Tikki spoke in a perfectly controlled voice. "Ma'am, if you an' th' rest o' th' folks 'ud like t' foller th' little gal, I'll see to it th' lights git put out proper."

At that moment the melee erupted, and the little band scurried through the door and corridor into the cold.

Jennifer moved to where she could look in a window. Tikki and his assailants were circling the room like desperate, savage animals, and she could see blood on Tikki's arm. Her attention was drawn away when Ray drove into the schoolyard with two other men, and when she looked back, the room was empty. Evidently they had fled at the sight of the flashing lights on Ray's car.

Ray and the two volunteers searched the premises but could find no one. After being assured it was safe, Jennifer and her students went back into the classroom to survey the ruins. Desks and chairs were overturned and scattered, but on closer inspection the damage was not as bad as Jennifer had expected. One chair was badly mangled, and there was blood smeared on the floor and furniture, but except for books and papers strewn everywhere, things seemed intact.

They could do little but make a big pile. And as Jennifer surveyed the scene, arms akimbo, she joked weakly, "I'll just tell Nola Mae that her first hour tomorrow morning is all planned for her. It'll be a game, like Shoe Scramble."

Actually, Nola Mae took the news of her ravaged classroom quite well. She had been in bed when Jennifer got home and didn't hear about it until breakfast.

"Ed Carlish told Ray he recognized the two men," Jennifer said, "but he didn't know their names."

"Probably a couple of goons from Calley Coal," said Nola Mae. "They tend to mind everybody else's business."

Jennifer chewed thoughtfully on her toast. "It just seemed so unfair, those two big bullies against Tikki, and nobody knows what happened after they ran out."

"Don't worry about Tikki Granger. From what I hear, he's well able to take care of himself. And what were Kenny and Joey doing all that time? Didn't they help him?"

"I don't know. Joey was so mad at Tikki before class, I doubt he helped him much. And Kenny doesn't look like he could get out of his own way."

"Well, when the chips are down, they'd stand by Tikki, I bet—or pay later!"

Jennifer spread the last dab of jelly. "When Tikki told us all to leave, he sounded so casual and unconcerned. The rest of us were scared to death. I'm not sure I could have walked out the door if the fight hadn't started right then. But we had no trouble moving after that!"

"Well," said Nola Mae as she rinsed out her cereal bowl, "it's probably a good thing my kids have all that stuff to sort through. They wouldn't be able to concentrate anyway. I'll be lucky to get them to settle down by mid-afternoon!"

13 That was the first really amicable conversation Jennifer had had with Nola Mae. But she didn't think much about it until a couple of days later when once again they found themselves talking.

It was the following Sunday afternoon, and Nola Mae, seldom home on weekends, was curled in her chair with a bowl of stew, reading.

"Have you ever thought," she asked without raising her head, "what it would be like to always be hungry? I mean really hungry, and even have to eat rotten food?"

A bit startled, Jennifer thought for a moment. "No, I guess I haven't."

"This is a book by Solzhenitsyn, and one of the themes that runs through all his writings is how much prisoners think about food and eating. I've got a whole list of places it pops up. Listen to this:

> During his hungry years in German captivity and Soviet prisons, Potapov had learned that eating is not something shameful, to be despised, but one of life's most delectable experiences, revealing the very essence of our existence.

"Here's another spot. They had just been served lunch:

> In the room that real silence fell which should always accompany eating. They thought: 'Here is a fat rich soup, a little thin to be sure, but with a meat flavor one can taste; I am putting into my mouth this spoonful, and this one, and this one, with the speck of fat and the white fibers of meat; the warm liquid will pass down my esophagus into my stomach; and my blood and muscles are already celebrating in anticipation of new reinforcements and new strength.'"

She began paging through the book. "There's another place . . . not that one . . . ah, here!

> 'Remember that thin, watery barley or the oatmeal porridge without a single drop of fat? Can you say you *eat* it? No. You commune with it, you take it like

a sacrament! Like the prana of the yogis. You eat it slowly; you eat it from the tip of the wooden spoon; you eat it absorbed entirely in the process of eating, in thinking about eating—and it spreads through your body like nectar. You tremble at the sweetness released from those overcooked little grains and the murky liquid they float in. And then—with hardly any nourishment—you go on living six months, twelve months. Can you really compare the crude devouring of a steak with this?'

"And then this line: '"Satiety depends not at all on *how much* we eat, but on *how* we eat. It's the same way with happiness, the very same."'"

The two women sat silent for a moment, thinking about what she had read. Jennifer took a deep breath and then laughed. "How do you feel now with that big bowl of stew in your lap?"

Nola Mae laughed, too. "I think I should set it on an altar with candles and eat it on my knees!"

Although Jennifer was scarcely aware of the connection, that conversation caused her to pay closer attention to Nola Mae's records, some of which were becoming like old friends—friends who spoke a deep emotional language. By comparison, her own gospel records were beginning to taste like the watery gruel of prison fare. *Have I been locked away and feeding on porridge all these years*, she wondered, *when I could have freely partaken of the rich literary and artistic fare of centuries?*

Of the poetry Nola Mae had given her—and the stack of photocopies in Jennifer's manila folder was growing—two in particular stirred her imagination. One began, "O Captain of the wars, whence won Ye so great scars?" and ended, "It is written, 'King of Kings, Lord of Lords.'" The other was similar and even more pleasurable when its elusive meaning finally came into focus, a portrait of the church in tribulation:

80

> O Lily of the King! low lies thy silver wing,
>> And long has been the hour of thine enqueening;
> And thy scent of Paradise on the night wind spill
>> its sighs,
> Nor any take the secrets of its meaning.
> O Lily of the King! I speak a secret thing,
>> O patience, most sorrowful of daughters,
> Lo, the hour is at hand for the troubling of the land,
> And red shall be the breaking of the waters.

She loved to read these two poems over and over, drinking in the imagery and riding on the rhythm.

Nola Mae also mentioned a piece called "The Hound of Heaven" by the same author, and when Jennifer looked puzzled, a touch of the old condescension came back into her voice. "You've *never* read 'The Hound of Heaven?' Good gracious!" But without further comment she dug out one of her books and placed it open on Jennifer's desk. "I won't have time to make a copy for you till next week. I'll be in Charleston all weekend. But you can keep this till then."

The poem was quite long, and though Jennifer understood little of it the first time through, the familiar pulsating rhythm and rhyming patterns carried her through "hearted casements," "Lady-Mother's vagrant tresses," and "the dust o' the mounded years" to the oasis of the repeated refrain:

> Still with unhurrying chase,
> And unperturbèd pace,
> Deliberate speed, majestic instancy
> Came on the following Feet.

But the end was clear, and its impact almost took her breath away.

> "Alack, thou knowest not
> How little worthy of any love thou art!
> Whom wilt thou find to love ignoble thee,
> Save Me, save only Me?

All which I took from thee I did but take,
  Not for thy harms,
But just that thou might'st seek it in My arms.
  All which thy child's mistake
Fancies as lost, I have stored for thee at home:
  Rise, clasp my hand, and come!"

  Halts by me that footfall:
  Is my gloom, after all,
Shade of His hand, outstretched caressingly?
  "Ah, fondest, blindest, weakest,
  I am He Whom thou seekest!
Thou dravest love from thee, who dravest Me."

As she reread this last section, tears filled her eyes. Was
this what she had been hiding from, showing Corey and
hoping he would tell her it wasn't fit to read? "Ah, fondest,
blindest, weakest—" that was she, locked in a narrow mold
of piety, afraid of somehow damaging God if she explored
the reaches of her freedom. *Freedom*—the word kept pop-
ping up everywhere, it seemed. The state motto displayed
prominently in her classroom, "Mountain Men Are Always
Free." And that verse in Nola Mae's song—

  When the mountain shall turn,
  When the victory is thine,
  Then my happiness dawns,
  Then shall freedom be mine.

Well, she'd need to think more about freedom, but not
now. She was exhausted and needed to go to bed early.
Tomorrow was Thursday, the day she dreaded most of all
the week. Who would show up for the class? Would the
"good guys" be scared off or the "bad guys" deterred by
the previous week's fracas? She fervently hoped they'd all
stay away.

But they didn't. Not all, anyhow. By class time, four had shown up. Only four, said Hope, but Jennifer dumbly resigned herself to the late arrival of the trio.

She had a terrible headache and would have given anything to be home in bed. The day had been difficult, and despite her early bedtime, she hadn't slept well the night before. She had awakened achy and irritable, and just getting through school had been a struggle.

A chill went through her now as the peculiar groan of the outer school door warned of another arrival. But only Tikki walked into the classroom and, with a smirking nod to Jennifer, sprawled noisily in a chair. Jim Baker made the mistake of asking if he'd gotten hurt the previous week, and Tikki rolled up his sleeve to show off his latest scar, a red, ugly gash on the side of his arm. "Hed t' hev sixty-nine stitches, crutches, an' a body cast, I did!"

"That so? It do look purty bad. Hurt much?" Jim asked sympathetically.

"Like hell an' then some. Why, hit took fourteen men t' hold me down while—"

"That will do, Tikki. I'm glad you were not seriously hurt—" Jennifer looked significantly at Jim "—and are able to be with us tonight. Now, if you'll turn to page seventy in your small book . . ." and she got the class into reading as quickly as possible to forestall further questions about Kenny and Joey.

The session was supremely difficult, and finally at eight o'clock Jennifer gave up. "You'll have to forgive me, class, but I have a bad headache, so we'll end early this week. Next time you'll get full measure, I promise." She gave the assignment, and they walked out together into the damp, raw night.

"Big storm comin', they say," remarked Ed. "Headin' right up toward us, an' we'll more'n likely git clobbered."

I hope so, thought Jennifer. *If it's big enough, they'll call off school.*

83

But by morning only a few flakes were drifting out of the leaden sky, and despite a dire forecast, school was on, at least for half a day. Nola Mae, determined to get to Charleston before the roads were impassable, had everything packed and in her car, ready to leave as soon as school let out. "You sound terrible!" she said to Jennifer, who was coughing and blowing. "Why don't you stay home? I know you don't want to waste a sick day if school's going to get out early anyway, but if ever you needed a day off, it's today."

"I thought of it, but there isn't a good sub available."

"Well, go to bed as soon as you get home. It'll be nice and quiet, and you can get a good rest."

By eleven that morning snow was falling with considerable determination, and the office announced that dismissal would be at 11:30. Jennifer was home by noon, feeling dreadful. Her sore throat and tight chest made it painful even to cough. She brewed herself a cup of camomile tea and sat down with "The Hound of Heaven." But her eyes were running too much to read. As she headed for the bedroom, another bad coughing spell made her decide to call Rusty. He was not yet home from school, so she left a message with his mother, asking him to pick up some cough medicine for her and bring it over. "I'll leave the door open and set some money on the table, Mrs. Chisholm. Rusty can just leave it there for me. I'd really appreciate it."

She dozed off but slept only fitfully, mostly because of the strange dreams, the kind that come with sickness and fever. She was running away, from what she didn't know, but there were faces—ugly, leering, triumphantly evil. She ran to this friend and that for help, but those from whom she most expected aid turned against her and were hard as stone. And echoing through the dreams were the words she had read over and over since the other night—"Still with unhurrying chase/ And unperturbèd pace . . ./ Came on the following Feet." She ran to Corey, but he stood with arms folded in frowning displeasure; to Ellen, who apologized and said she had her own children to care for; to Nola Mae, who laughed hysterically and ran off to Charleston. She tried Rosalie, but the little girl couldn't hear her pleas, intent on making a doll that looked like Tikki. The Feet came on, and there was nowhere else to turn. . . .

Jennifer heaved herself up in bed, heart pounding wildly, and reached over for another sip of the now-cold tea to soothe her throat. As she lay back, trying to erase the effect of the dream, thumping and stomping on the front porch announced the arrival of genuine aid.

"Is that you, Rusty?" she called hoarsely as she heard the door shut.

"It's all right, ma'am. It's Tikki."

| 14 | *It's all right, ma'am. It's Tikki.* Jennifer said the words over to herself. *It's all right. . . .* |

If the Devil himself were out there saying it, it couldn't be any less all right. What was she to do now? Get up or stay in bed? The phone was a million miles away, and if it suited him that she not use it, he'd rip it off the wall. She coughed painfully and rolled over on her side till the spasm passed, so utterly miserable that crying seemed the only possible response to his plaguing.

While she was thus contemplating the frayed end of her rope, Tikki walked on in and set something on the kitchen table. He peered briefly through the open door of the bedroom but said nothing and went instead to tend the wood

85

stove. Only after he had shed his enormous sheepskin jacket and unpacked his bundles did he come into the bedroom.

Jennifer hadn't moved. She lay with tears rolling onto the pillow, all pretense aside. With no choice left but to deal with him head-on, she looked up into his impassive face and said, "Please go away, Tikki. *Please*—I can't—"

"Shut up," he commanded, and put a cool hand on her forehead.

"But—" and another coughing spasm wracked her.

"Be still. Jes' lie there an' don't say nothin'. Don't *think* nothin'. Jes' be still." His hands, surprisingly gentle, eased her back. By now she was crying in earnest, and after giving her a tissue from the box by her bed, he went into the bathroom and brought back a wet washcloth and wiped her face.

"Hev you slep' any?"

"A little."

"You taken anything?"

"Medicine, you mean? Just aspirin. I asked Rusty—"

"I know. I got it. Now, jes' lie still an' rest while I fix you somethin'."

He went out, and she lay looking up at the ceiling and listening to the snow lashing against the window. Along with head and throat throbbing and each breath feeling like the stab of a knife, she now had Tikki Granger trying to play Good Samaritan, probably with the intention of fattening her up to have for his dinner. She resolved to pretend she was sleeping when he came back.

But it didn't work. Ignoring her closed eyes, he made her sit up and take a cup of soup that tasted strange but seemed soothing, and a vile-tasting potion that felt good on her throat. After that, she didn't have to fake anything and slept till the middle of the night. And shortly after her first waking cough, Tikki was at her side.

He gave her some more of the potion he had brewed up, then asked, "Does it he'p any?"

She nodded. "It's soothing. What is it?"

But he shook his head. "Might make y' feel better, but it ain't apt t' he'p th' sickness. Not much will when it's this bad."

She watched him as he stared out the window into the blackness of the storm with a serious, almost sad, expression on his face.

"Tikki, why are you doing this?"

He continued to stare, almost as if he hadn't heard her. "Well," he finally said, lightness returning to his face, "ev'r so often I take a spell that gets me a-hankerin' t' pay off m' debts. Prob'ly won't last too long, 's long as th' storm, mebbe."

Jennifer reflected on that cold windy night in October. "You don't owe me anything, Tikki. You wouldn't let me do anything for you!"

"Well," he smiled, "mebbe I know what it's like t' hev a headache. Any rate, you're too sick t' be here alone in th' middle of a blizzard."

"Somebody else could come—"

"Who? Half th' town's sick. An' t'ain't likely Lover Boy 'ud put hisself out t' come over on a night like this, an'—" overriding Jennifer's protest, "an' even if he did, he wouldn't come in th' house with you here alone, t' say nothin' of bein' in bed. Now me," he grinned, "I ain't encumbered with any sech twitches. . . . 'Course there's Miss Sadie McCusker, hale 'n hardy. Th' Devil sees to it she don't ever git sick. She'd keep fine comp'ny fer you. I c'd go heist 'er on my back an' fetch her over, if y' like."

Jennifer laughed but started coughing again. Tikki immediately stood up and put a strong but gentle hand on her shoulder as if willing ease upon her. "No more talk. Jes' rest an' sleep if y' kin. I'll be right outside th' door if y' need me."

Saturday morning dawned reluctantly with neither Jennifer nor the storm any better. Her coughing and wheezing and blowing had become so painful that she was in tears often. Tikki's nostrum helped a great deal and gave her an hour or so of rest each time she took it, but he would only give it to her every three hours.

By now she had relaxed about his being there. She couldn't have gotten a better nurse if she had chosen one herself. He attended to her needs very capably, with little talk or fuss. For some mysterious inner moving known only to himself, Tikki was all she could ever ask for in an attendant. Though sometimes gruff, especially when she tried to get up by herself and almost fainted, he was unfailingly gentle and comforting.

Raskolnikov didn't fare as well, however. Being one of the few truly friendly and impartial cats, he tried with persistent determination to win over this stranger; but before long, an exasperated Tikki grabbed him by the scruff of the neck and heaved him into the pantry, dumping some cat food on the floor next to his bowl of water. Raskolnikov showed uncommon good sense by keeping still after that, probably with a prudent eye on the outside door as the next portal through which he might be cast.

The angry storm worried Tikki. He wandered restlessly from one window to another looking out at the curtain of white being sculpted by the unrelenting wind. At midmorning, Rusty came to the house on snowshoes and reported that nothing was moving in town. The road crew had given up trying to keep the streets open until after the storm had moved on. Because of drifting, the amount of snow that had fallen was difficult to determine, but the best estimate put it at twelve or thirteen inches and still coming strong.

Tikki looked grim at this news. "She's got t' hev a doctor, but they's no way. Not in this storm. Hit 'ud take a bulldozer t' break through that pass, an' even then it 'ud be blowed in afore a car c'd git through. I cain't even git a call out. Nuthin' but busy signals, or nuthin' 'tall."

He stood thinking a moment, then turned to the boy. "Rusty, y' got t' go to th' drug store an' see what Frank Stanley kin git fer her in this kind of emergency. Tell him her throat an' chest are so bad she's hevin' trouble breathin', an' she's got a pretty high fever. Tell 'im t' call a doctor if he kin git through, but if he cain't, t' send somethin' over anyhow. She's mighty sick."

Shortly after Rusty had slogged back down the drive, bent against the wind, Hilda Smith came by, saying she would take over. On Tikki's rejection of that offer, she demanded entrance to make sure Jennifer was all right. But Tikki sent her packing with characteristic charm. When he went in to Jennifer, who had heard the altercation, she received him with a whispered, "Thank you."

As he sat in the chair beside her bed, she looked at him in mute appeal for something to relieve her wretchedness. "Not fer another half hour. Then I'll git you some, with a little soup, too."

She tried to smile through her swollen and blotchy face. "Good thing I'm not into drugs. I'd be a hopeless case." Tikki frowned, his face becoming even more inscrutable. She moved her head restlessly. "If I didn't feel so awful . . ."

"If you like, I c'd put a record on. Would that he'p or be a bother?"

Her eyes brightened. "Yes. Please! My records are in that box in the corner. You'd probably like those better than Nola Mae's, but she wouldn't mind if you played hers."

"Hmph—as if I care what Nola Mae minds!"

89

As she heard the familiar strains of *Appalachian Spring*, Jennifer was glad he had by-passed her records. She lay with eyes closed, letting the music wash gently over her. About halfway through, she thought of the irony of what she was hearing—the rollicking dance of a spring festival against the tumult outside tirelessly clawing at the house. The music seemed frail and impotent against such obdurate strength, but even as she listened, she sensed that the ultimate power lay in the music, not the storm, and the music made mockery of the violence without.

"Dance, then, wherever you may be,
I am the Lord of the Dance," said He.

A coughing fit overtook her, and she hunched over, wheezing and gasping, frightened by how weak she felt in its grip. *Jesus, are you Lord of the cough, too?*

Tikki came in with his medicaments in hand and quickly set them down when he saw her distress. After helping her sit up and propping her with additional pillows, he started to rub more liniment on her throat, then set it aside.

"I know you kin hardly wait till I put more o' this on, but you'll hev t' eat first," he smiled, knowing she hated the pungency that made her eyes stream.

Eating was difficult and every swallow a major hurdle. Had she been alone, she wouldn't have made the effort, but Tikki persisted, and she got down a half cup or so of soup. The potion, though also hard to take, promised enough respite to motivate her to drink it.

Rusty came back with some capsules, saying Frank hadn't thought they'd do a whole lot of good. He had not been able to get through to a doctor and didn't dare risk giving her anything stronger.

Tikki swore grimly and then said, "You go back an' tell

Frank that th' law's got a long arm, but conscience, if somethin' happens t' Jennifer, is got an even longer one. Tell him t' chew on that fer a spell an' come up with what he thinks a good doctor'd prescribe. She's bad an' gittin' worse, an' they ain't all that much further t' git."

The afternoon wore on. When Jennifer woke, Tikki put on another record, a Tchaikovsky symphony. He came into her room where they listened together in silence. Tikki's face reflected the melancholy music with a look of infinite sadness. As Jennifer watched him, her eyes tracing the braid on his shirt and the jagged scar along his right thumb, it was almost as though she were hearing music for the first time, hearing and seeing in Tikki and feeling well up within herself the sadness of countless generations of men and women who knew struggle and failure and death and loss.

She had come to realize that music was not just something to enjoy in off moments. It was a profound statement of life, reaching down to the inner depths of the human soul to express the otherwise inexpressible, the joys and sorrows and longings and magnificent strivings of the human heart. And Russian music seemed particularly eloquent with its poignancy, its rollicky, robust dances, but especially its soul-wrenching grief. It brought to mind Nola Mae's readings of the prisoners' solemn attention to food, the heart-cry of an oppressed people through many centuries of suffering. As she listened to the grimly triumphant climax to the third movement and the first weeping chords of the final one, tears of vicarious sorrow mingling with self-pity rolled onto her pillow.

Tikki, lost in his own deliberations, seemed oblivious, but the emotion of the music began to affect him, and with a shudder he stood up. "We don't need that right now!" Seeing Jennifer's tears, he stopped and then almost ran out of the room.

He jerked the arm from the record with a violent scratch that made Jennifer wince. When he came back, she croaked, "Nola Mae will—"

"Damn Nola Mae and her records! I shoulda knowed better'n t' put that on."

"It's all right. I liked it," she managed to say. His anger upset her, and she tried to raise herself, but just then they heard footsteps on the porch.

It was Ray Windle, who looked quizzically at Tikki's haggard face. "Seems like you've had quite a day. How is she?"

"Bad. Real bad. She needs a doc right away. What're th' chances?"

Ray shook his head. "Not good. It's supposed to quit by morning, but we've got over twenty inches of hard-drift snow out there right now. About the worst storm I ever seen in these parts. And th' likelihood of their gittin' th' Jensen road open before noon tomorrow is pretty slim."

"She could be dead by noon! Ain't there some way t' git word out—phone, radio—anything?"

Ray's concern deepened. "She really that bad?"

"She ain't dyin' yit, but by t'morrow noon . . ."

"I'll work on it, Tikki. I'll do everything I can. D' you need anything we *can* get? Have enough food?"

"I bin tryin' t' git Frank t' send over some real medicine, but he won't jostle th' law none. Ain't a gamblin' man, he says."

"Yeah, he talked to me about it, and I can't make him do it. He's not a doctor and don't have a doctor's knowledge, and—"

"He knows full well what'll do what, an' c'd prob'ly make as good a guess as any doctor could over th' phone. He'll gamble with Jennifer's life, but not with his business! If 'twas his wife dyin', he'd do somethin'!"

"I'll see what I can do, but I can't work a miracle. I'm

sorry. I wish there was more I could do."

Tikki nodded with a sigh of resignation. "Thanks fer comin' by." And with anxious weariness lining his face, he watched Ray snowshoe into the night, the swinging pinpoint of his flashlight quickly swallowed by blackness.

15 Sunday morning dawned clear and bright on the pristine whiteness of twenty-five inches of snow. In some high places, the ground had been scoured clean by the wind; elsewhere, drifts swelled to over six feet or hung curled in frozen waves.

Throughout the town, children left their homes and leapt out into the drifts with an exuberance that knew none of the exigencies of shoveling snow or uncovering buried firewood. They laughed and played with an innate appreciation for the infinite variety of uses for snow: sliding, rolling, sculpting, shuffling, skiing, lying, throwing, excavating, building, tossing, packing, flopping, eating, admiring, tunneling, leaping, and on and on wherever fertile imagination led.

Randy Lindel floundered through a drift in his driveway on his way to the house. Weary, eyes bloodshot, he stomped and brushed the snow off his pantlegs.

Ellen was in the kitchen, wrapped in a warm robe, the residual effects of illness still heavy upon her. "Where did you go? I heard you get up and go to the door, but I guess I must've fallen back to sleep. The next thing I knew, it was morning and you were gone."

Randy gave a tired sigh and poured himself a cup of coffee. "I've been out plowing."

"Plowing! You've never plowed before!"

"I have now. And believe me, I got a lotta respect for the guys who do it all the time. Never again will I complain about a sloppy job!" He flopped into a chair and rubbed his head. "I'm sorry. I should've left a note for you."

"Where were you—in town here?"

"Mostly on Jensen Road." He paused. "You see, there's a problem. Ray came by and said we had to open up as close to Jensen as we could, as soon as we could. Jennifer's sick, and they've got to get her to the hospital."

"Oh, no! What's wrong?"

"Well, I guess it's flu, but real bad. Ray says she's having trouble breathing."

"Who's with her—Nola Mae?"

He gave her a crooked smile. "You won't believe this . . . Tikki Granger."

"No! I don't believe it!"

"What's more, Ray says Tikki's taking care of her as well—probably better—than anyone else could. But nobody's been able to get ahold of a doctor, and Frank won't go out on a limb to give her anything that might help."

"Well, I can talk Frank Stanley out of that nonsense! How bad is she?"

Randy pondered the effect of his words. "Tikki was talking last night about the possibility of her dying, but Ray didn't actually see her himself, so he can't say for sure."

Ellen began to cry. "I'll get bundled up and go over. I'm not that bad and—"

Randy reached over and grabbed her arm. "I was afraid you'd say that. Now listen to reason, Ellen. Number one, you'd get all the way over there and Tikki wouldn't let you through the door . . . you can bet on that. Number two, there's nothing you can do that's not already being done. Ray says that for some unknown reason, Tikki is going all out for her. I don't know why, but he's taking good care of her and probably knows more mountain remedies than the rest of us put together. And number three, you'd put yourself back in bed, and what help could you be to Jennifer then?" Ellen was weeping again. "I know you feel bad, hon. I do, too. That's why I was out all night banging away at those drifts. You can't get through with just the light equipment we had, but Ray *made* us get through. When we were stuck, we shoveled, Ray right along with the rest of us. The best thing you can do is pray that they get some heavy machines up in that pass right away!"

As they talked, Rusty was making his way up Jennifer's driveway.

In ten minutes he shuffled back down the drive with all the speed he could muster, thoroughly frightened by the look of explosive anger in Tikki's gaunt, haggard face and by the ghastly sound of labored breathing coming from behind the closed door of the bathroom. The smell of steam and liniment had been everywhere, and Rusty took in great gulps of cold, fresh air, glad to be outdoors once again.

But he would have to go back, and he fervently hoped to have some medicine from Frank. "She's dyin'!" Tikki had rasped. "She's dyin'! *Git that through his skairt little head!* An' it's got t' be in a form she kin take—liquid or a syringe. Now, *go!*" he thundered, and Rusty hustled.

But Frank had been pressed into plowing as a relief man for the night crew. So Rusty turned out Tully the bartender, who had just completed his shift of plowing, to drive him out to where the men were working. He finally found Ray, who listened in tired silence to Rusty's report and without a word went to his CB to track down Frank.

A half hour later, Frank had been transported to the drugstore, and Rusty was soon running down the middle of Main Street, package in one hand, snowshoes tucked under the other, more than a little apprehensive as to how Tikki would receive the medicine.

His fears were well-founded. Tikki ripped open the bag and stared in disbelief at the bottle of large capsules. His swearing began softly, then gathered intensity as he hurled the bottle against the kitchen wall where it splintered and scattered capsules everywhere.

Rusty sidled toward the door, but Tikki's stentorian voice nailed him to the spot. "Don't you dare leave! I'm gonna need you! It's her only chance!"

Suddenly a new thought directed his attention to the floor. He reached down for one of the capsules and twisted it open, studying the powdery contents. With what might pass for a smile, he emptied two more into a small dish and, adding a tablespoon of water, stirred the mixture carefully. After tasting a drop, he carried dish and spoon into the steamy bathroom, with another stern warning to Rusty not to leave.

Rusty wandered around, closely inspecting the room and each item in it, trying to block out the awful gasping and choking coming from behind the door. He didn't have long to wait, however. In just a few minutes Tikki came out, drenched with perspiration, grinding his teeth in frustration and rage. "It's too late, it's too damned *late!* She cain't swaller nothin'!"

He paced the room, then sat at the desk with head in hands, staring with unseeing eyes at the pages of the open book before him. Finally he stood, face white and drawn. "I got t' do it. They's no gittin' around it. An' you're gonna help!" He strode past the trembling lad into the bedroom and spread a clean sheet over the one already on the bed and gave some clean pillowcases to Rusty. "After I git her outta the bathroom, take th' cases off th' pillows an' put these on 'em."

He lifted the limp form, securely wrapped in a cocoon of blankets, and carried it to the bed. When Rusty followed, he stopped in his tracks. "Tikki! She's dead!" Indeed, Jennifer looked like death, her skin pallid and turning blue, eyes glazed and staring, facial muscles straining in a horrible grimace as she struggled for each breath.

"No, she ain't—not yet. An' we're gonna fight right down t' th' wire!" Tikki wiped the cold sweat off Jennifer's face and moistened her parched lips with a wet cloth. As he sat looking at her, he began to tremble and buried his face on the bed. The only sound in the whole house was the rasping, erratic gasps of the sick woman. He leaned back and drew several deep breaths, his eyes pleading for her to be better. But she was not. Finally he stood, his face white but fortified with a look of resolve. "Stay here an' watch her."

He was back in a few minutes with a pan of boiling water in which lay a small, razor-sharp penknife and a hollow wooden tube about two inches long. Rusty had seen Tikki working on that tube when he had come the first time this morning, and now he looked at it with curiosity. "Whatcha gonna do with that?"

Tikki, busy collecting cotton, bandage material, and clean rags, didn't respond right away. But after surveying his stock with satisfaction, he faced Rusty squarely and drew a shaky breath. "Her throat's swelled so bad it's squeezin' her windpipe shut an' she's gittin' no air in her lungs. I got t' cut a hole in her windpipe so's she kin breathe, an' you gotta hold her so she don't move. If she does, an' th' knife slips, it c'd—"

But Rusty's legs had turned to jelly, and he bolted for the door. Tikki was on him in an instant, snapping him around and slamming him up against the wall. "You're gonna hold her, an' you ain't gonna let go till I say so!" He held his face within inches of the boy's.

Rusty licked his white lips. "What if I faint?"

"You faint, an' you jes' better see to it you don't wake up while I'm around. Is it clear in yer head now jes' what I expect of you?"

Rusty nodded solemnly.

"An' you know jes' what to expect of me if you goof up?"

He nodded again, eyes wide.

"Well, then—" and he eased off of the boy, "we got us a job t' do."

Anger had given Tikki strength, and he set about positioning Jennifer for the operation. With one pillow under the small of her back and two under her shoulders, her head was tipped back sharply. Next, he sat on the bed beside her to test out his own hold on her, his legs over her right arm and left arm clamping her head to his thigh. He instructed Rusty how to hold her other arm and shoulder and warned him to expect blood to spurt or even spray quite a distance. Rusty said nothing, but swallowed hard several times. Tikki then opened the top buttons of Jennifer's robe and gown and tucked a clean cloth around her neck.

Satisfied with the arrangements, he put a pillow under her head and went out to scrub his hands. He was almost done when Rusty cried out, "She ain't breathin' much, an' she's turnin' black!"

Tikki ran in, hands still dripping. "Yes. It's time. Take th' pillow out from under her head . . . easy. An' git a good holt on her—an' yerself."

He swabbed her neck with alcohol, and perspiration poured from his ashen face as he took his position on the bed and picked up the knife. His breath coming almost in sobs, he wiped his dripping face on his sleeve and, with only a slight hesitation, slowly and carefully inserted the knife into her neck and opened a half-inch slit that hissed and spewed blood everywhere. Jennifer writhed and heaved beneath them, but with Rusty's death grip on her, her neck remained reasonably still. As the hole widened, she began pulling air into her lungs in great drafts, a sound that was music to Tikki's ears. He swabbed the hole with gauze, and when the bleeding had nearly stopped, he inserted the little wooden tube, watching carefully to see that air exchange was still taking place. Satisfied, he eased himself off her arm and was pleased to see color returning to her face.

He looked over at the boy. Rusty was holding on for all he was worth, his gelatinous body gagging and retching.

"It's all over. You kin come up fer air now." Rusty just rolled his head from side to side. "Leastwise, git off her arm so it don't git gangrene."

As Rusty slowly pulled himself off the bed and gagged again at the sight of the blood, Tikki spoke sharply. "Stand up an' git aholt o' yerself! They's still more t' do." A look of terror came over the lad. "I want you t' hunt up a station wagon an' two able-bodied men an' be back here inside an hour. An' that mountain had better be open by now!"

Within twenty minutes a plow was working its way up Hazel Lane, and soon afterward Randy and Wes Bishop backed a station wagon to within ten feet of the front porch. Using the canvas stretcher they had brought, they carefully bundled Jennifer onto a cradle of pillows in the back of the wagon.

Tikki sat beside Jennifer all the way to the Jensen hospital, but as soon as they arrived and the emergency crew had eased her onto a rolling stretcher, he took off at a run, staggering and stumbling like a drunken man.

Inside, the medical staff examined the surgical handiwork with amazement. "I've seen tracheotomies done by a doctor that weren't as good as this. You sure this guy isn't a surgeon?"

Randy shook his head. "He's the most unlikely person in all the world to do any of what he's done in the past forty-eight hours! He did what none of the rest of us would've dared, and he saved her life!"

16 Nola Mae's weekend in Charleston with Jeremy Tybolt had been less than satisfying. At first, being snowbound had seemed a lark, but as Saturday wore on, Jeremy grew restless and curt, and the couple that did finally break through to toast the storm with them brought along their own tedium. They were plowed out by Sunday, but there was nothing to do. Movie theaters had been closed and cultural events cancelled because of the storm, and how much time can you spend in a restaurant?

And so Nola Mae returned home relatively early Sunday evening in none too good a mood for the surprises ahead of her. First was the dark house, then a strong medicinal smell and chilly where it should have been warm. The odor reminded her that Jennifer had had a cold. Now, with a stab of alarm, she wondered whether Jennifer was in bed, too sick even to tend the stove. She called out but received no answer.

Flipping on the lights and slipping off her snowy boots, she walked toward Jennifer's bedroom, surprised at how cold the floor felt to her stocking feet.

But the biggest surprise of all awaited her in the bedroom. Blood . . . chaos . . . Jennifer had been attacked and dragged off!

Nola Mae screamed and ran to the phone, hurting her feet on capsules scattered over the kitchen floor, but the phone was dead. Struck with horror, panic rose within her as she looked at the pantry door near the phone. Had

Jennifer's body been stuffed in there? Was the assailant there also, waiting for *her*? She ran toward the front door, where she frantically and clumsily struggled into her boots.

Slamming the door behind her, she slipped on the steps and landed in a heap on the ground. By now crying hysterically, she got to the car, only to realize her keys were still in the house. She fled down Hazel Lane to the Potters' house, where she pounded on the front door for several minutes as Ed made his way to the door.

Not until Mrs. Potter had insisted she drink a cup of tea was Nola Mae able to tell them what the trouble was. The old couple calmed and reassured her but could shed no light on what had become of Jennifer. They had noticed that the plow came by unusually early for this severe a storm, but most of their day had been spent in their cozy sitting room on the side of the house away from the street.

The Potters were kind and helpful, and Ed offered to go back with Nola Mae to check out the house. Since she could think of no better option—walking to Ray Windle's house was out of the question—she agreed.

But back at the house they could find nothing. Nothing but the cat, who was exceedingly grateful for release from his pantry prison. The kitchen, bathroom, and linen closet were all a mess, and not a pillow was to be found in the entire house. But their search uncovered neither body nor intruder, so Ed built a fire for her and left. Nola Mae had hoped he would suggest that she stay the night with them, but he didn't. So she was left alone with the unsolved mystery of what had become of Jennifer.

The missing pillows puzzled her. Nola Mae's, Jennifer's, even the small decorator pillows had disappeared. And the blood. A cold doesn't normally cause bleeding, and certainly not to that extent.

She looked more closely at the clutter in the kitchen, first sweeping up the capsules and broken bottle shards. Someone other than Jennifer had been around, she was sure of that. There were unfamiliar bottles and bags on the kitchen table, and Jennifer would never have left such a mess, sick or no.

In the bathroom another clue emerged. The raised toilet seat and spatter around the rim of the bowl clearly spoke of a man's presence over quite a period of time. Curiouser and curiouser. Jennifer? A man? As sick as she was? Corey came to mind, but she dismissed the idea as highly unlikely; with Jennifer in the house alone, even on her deathbed, he would never have come in.

Then she found her Tchaikovsky record with its fatal scratch still on the turntable. "How *could* she?" she exploded to no one in particular.

Sounds of stomping on the porch set her heart pounding in panic. The knock came before she had time to get out of sight, but the cheerful wave she saw through the door window seemed to indicate friend rather than foe.

She opened the door cautiously, then swung it wide in exasperation to let in Wesley Bishop, arms laden with blankets and pillows.

"Evenin', ma'am." He came through the door, grinning foolishly. "Thought I'd bring these back t'night when someone 'ud be here t' receive 'em." He was clearly tickled that his errand had gained him a precious audience with Nola Mae.

Good heavens! Was it Wesley who had been here with Jennifer? She'd need to fumigate the place!

"That's very kind of you, but where is Jennifer? And why is there blood all over everything?"

"Don't you *know?* Ain't you heard *nothin'* about it?"

"No—I haven't. I just got home a short while ago. And the phone is dead."

Wesley swelled with the importance of being the initial bearer of bad tidings and shifted from one foot to the other.

102

"Well, ma'am, it's like this . . . mebbe we c'd set down while I tell you."

"I think not," was Nola Mae's frosty reply. But undaunted, Wesley went on with his story, bringing in as much detail as he could remember or invent.

Nola Mae's anger rose as she listened, and the difficulty of dislodging Wesley once he finished only served to increase it. When finally alone once again, she flew into her own private tempest that included kicking furniture, throwing her ruined record, and beating on the bloodied pillows. Her ire appeared to be directed toward a number of things and people—Wesley for having the audacity to visit her at this time of night; Tikki for doing a heroic thing that was totally out of character and for messing up the house so badly; the phone company for letting her down in a moment of crisis; but mostly, she was furious with Jennifer for getting so sick that everything—the house, the town, the whole weekend—had been bent out of shape, and especially for causing Nola Mae tears of concern and pain and worry—even now.

17 Jennifer lay in her bed at the hospital thoroughly annoyed with Corey and with herself. She had said things she shouldn't have and had hurt him, and tomorrow she would have to apologize. But still, she couldn't believe he had actually proposed to her here in this four-bed hospital room with its unbroken parade of patients, visitors, nurses, aides, and cleaning ladies. Even discounting the unromantic setting, she was barely able to sit up and talk, hardly a condition in which to give serious consideration to a marriage proposal. His insensitivity had made her angry, and after he

103

left she had quietly cried into the pillow.

But now in thinking it over, she began to see a little more clearly the shape of the urgent feelings within Corey that had prompted his untimely proposal. Her close call had thoroughly frightened him, and the magnitude of the effort necessary to save her life—in which he had had no part—overwhelmed him. Several of the men of the church had been involved one way or another in the assault on the snow-choked highway, and for Corey to be beholden to so many for so precious a thing was a new experience.

And Tikki was on his mind. As they had talked about what the man had done, Jennifer could see that Corey felt both grateful and envious. She realized now her mistake in emphasizing Tikki's gentleness and competence. She still looked back with awe on that aspect of the drama, but Corey didn't like to hear about it. He kept saying how grateful he was, but in almost the same breath carefully brought out the importance of not confusing gratitude with approval of the man's sinful lifestyle.

And thinking through all this, Jennifer realized the problem at the heart of it all: Tikki had done what Corey with all his efficiency and drive could never have done. His mother might have, but not Corey. If he had been there with no one else to help, certainly Corey would have entered the house and cared for her; he would have prayed and cast out demons and claimed God's resurrecting power; he would even have been kind to the cat. But Corey would have been powerless, both by knowledge and inclination, to perform the life-saving actions that Tikki had taken. Jennifer knew this, *and Corey knew this*. And the implications of his impotence put him at a psychological disadvantage. Corey liked—needed—to be in control, and he did not care to be beholden to a man like Tikki Granger, or to be seen to disadvantage in comparison with him.

So he had proposed to Jennifer. But instead of strengthening his position, it had simply annoyed her, and he had gone away feeling hurt and angry and terribly insecure—all unusual emotions for him.

In the days that followed, Jennifer had many visitors, including a couple of strangers from Jensen who had helped to clear the roads and stopped by to wish her well. Nola Mae, to Jennifer's surprise, came several times, but explained in off-hand fashion that she was in town for other purposes and thought she'd drop in just to say hello. Rusty visited often, sometimes walking over from the high school in Jensen and hoping that someone from Clevis would be there to give him a ride home. In his mind, all the trauma and distress of the weekend had faded into oblivion, and he swaggered about telling and retelling his version of the crisis. Jennifer had already been apprised by Ray and Randy of the vital role Rusty had played as go-between and medical assistant, so she had no trouble heaping on praise and gratitude as a reward.

Even Joey Hamlin came, and Jennifer was touched by his show of concern. She took care not to foster any mis-understanding of her feelings toward him but thanked him warmly for coming.

But the person she most hoped would appear did not. No one had seen Tikki since Sunday noon when he lurched away from the hospital. It was to him she most wanted to express gratitude. She owed him her life, but there was more, much more, she wanted to say.

Thinking is hard in a hospital and, next to sleeping, probably the most difficult thing to do during the too-brief interludes of peace amidst the flurry of blood-letting, poking, and temperature-taking. But Jennifer used the little thinking time available trying to sort out her own feelings— about Tikki, about Corey, about her own life in view of her brush with death. She had apologized to Corey for the things she had said in response to his marriage proposal and had suggested in a way he was able to accept that she not make a decision on so weighty a matter until things were back to normal.

But often in quiet moments her mind would slip back to the way Tikki had seen to her needs—*as if he really cared*. She had been only dimly aware of Sunday's events, but the one thing that had been burned into her mind was the anguish in Tikki's eyes as he willed each breath into her tortured body. Again she saw him listening to the Tchaikovsky symphony, unwittingly allowing her to observe the secret pain and sadness he had kept so well hidden. Tikki Granger was obviously a man scarred by more than knife blades.

Yes, Corey was justified in his concern. She was emotionally entangled with Tikki; she couldn't help but be. She kept trying to be objective, to look at the sort of person he was, at least on the surface.. Uncouth, rough, shiftless, given to violence and dissolution. But the other side of the coin had revealed courage, resourcefulness, gentleness, and skill in nursing. And an appreciation for music of which even Nola Mae would approve.

Jennifer was convinced that there was far more to Tikki than any of them had seen, but what it all added up to she couldn't begin to say. She only knew that for reasons known to himself alone, he had turned the kind of person he was to good effect and had held on to her life with fully as much determination as he had ever displayed in his more iniquitous pursuits.

She kept returning to her initial impression of him as someone akin to Samson. The biblical Samson might not have been quite that dirty, but the wildness part fit well enough. The Lord was able to use Samson, even with his colorful and free-wheeling lifestyle. Might not Tikki in his own way . . . ?

Knowing full well the dangers of the ground she trod,

she casually threw out a question or two on Samson to Corey. He looked at her sharply. "I hope you're not trying to equate Tikki Granger with Samson!"

"Oh, no," she replied hastily. "But now that you mention it, there are a few similarities."

"Like what?"

"Well, in looks—they both have long hair—"

"That's about it, though. Samson was a servant of God."

"Was he really? Or did God use him like He would an unwitting club?"

"I don't know what you're talking about, Jennifer. Samson was one of the judges of Israel, aligned with Jehovah's people. Tikki is a godless reprobate and can do nothing in his present state that would please the Lord."

"Was God pleased when Samson married a Philistine woman? How about his visits to prostitutes? And the whole Delilah episode? About the most godly thing he accomplished in his whole life was to pray for strength to kill himself. Read it yourself . . . all he ever did was kill people. Tikki at least saves lives."

Corey was silent as he reached for his Bible and read through the four pertinent chapters in the Book of Judges. When he finished, he sat pondering.

This was the first time Jennifer had caught him on a biblical matter, and her eyes twinkled. "Not exactly a prime candidate for your board of deacons, is he?"

Corey frowned. "In answer to your first question, yes, God was pleased when he married the Philistine woman. It says in 14:4 that this was from the Lord. It was God's purpose to destroy the Philistines who had set themselves against Him, and He used Samson to accomplish this."

"An unwitting club?"

"No—not unwitting. He knew very well what his job was and was eager to do it."

"Oh, Corey! You can't mean to tell me you approve of the way Samson went about it—his lifestyle and all."

"Of course not. But if you're trying to get me to say that because Tikki Granger saved your life he's as good or better than Samson, you're wasting your breath. Samson was a judge of Israel under God and led the people for twenty years. That's the important principle—his heart was inclined toward the Lord."

"Well, he certainly had strange ways of showing it. If Tikki suddenly began knocking heads together down at Tully's and throwing people out the door, would that convince you of his godliness?"

"I think we'd better change the subject."

"Apart from Tikki altogether, I just want to know how God can use a disobedient, immoral, violent man like Samson, whose whole life runs counter to everything taught in the Bible—both Old and New Testaments. If he showed up at Clevis Baptist, you'd . . . well, I was going to say you'd throw him out in five minutes, but it might take a little longer." She giggled. "And I'd want to know pretty quick whose side he was on!"

18   When Jennifer first got home from the hospital, Nola Mae seemed nervous and edgy about the possibility of having to provide invalid care. But Jennifer was making a good recovery, and even with a bothersome cough and having to rest a lot, she could look after herself very well. As in the hospital, many people stopped by either to chat or to bring food. After the first three days at home, she asked Corey to tell folks she had enough food to last a month. Ellen came in every day to do

dishes or laundry and see that she had proper care.

"You're spoiling me!" Jennifer complained. "By the time I go back to school I'll be so fat and lazy, everyone will think I've been pretending to be sick!"

"You just show them the pretty little scar on your neck. That's no fake!" Ellen's brow creased every time she thought of that dreadful weekend.

Jennifer received a card from Corey's folks, an expensive but antiseptic expression of solicitude: "With sincere regards and best wishes for your rapid recovery." There was no note with it, nothing but their signature, "Murray and Adelle Witham." But a few days later, a beautiful bouquet of large yellow roses came to the house with a note attached that read, "You are much in our thoughts and prayers, and we hope to hear good news soon. Cordially, Murray and Adelle." With a touch of irritation, Jennifer wondered just what shape they were expecting the good news to take.

Lietta Wickens, the librarian, came with some books she thought Jennifer might like to read. She also brought news that Tikki was back in town, ugly and mean as ever. "Frieda Copp told me just this morning that she had heard from Hilda that when he came in for groceries, he deliberately— that's Hilda's word—*deliberately* stumbled into a fancy display of cans Hubert had just finished stacking. Hubert hollered at him, of course, but without a word Tikki threw a ten-dollar bill onto the pile and just walked out. Hubert was furious. Ten dollars doesn't build the stack back up again, you know."

Jennifer knew by this time that the Smiths' personal vendetta against Tikki colored all they said about him. Anything he did they would interpret as "mean," and an honest misstep in the store would be dealt with far differently than if someone besides Tikki had done it. She thought it a good sign that he had paid for the damage and said nothing.

During her period of recuperation, Jennifer had plenty

of time to read. She looked through the stack Lietta had brought from the library but was vexed to see only children's books. However, not finding anything in Nola Mae's collection that she cared to tackle, she returned to the children's fare and looked more closely. There was *Peter Pan* with delightful illustrations. That might be fun. She had seen a movie version or two but couldn't remember ever having read the book. And then another little volume, *The Little Prince* by Saint-Exupéry, caught her eye. These books might not be so bad after all. At least they wouldn't tax her mind.

But they did, in ways she hadn't anticipated. After finishing *The Little Prince*, she sat and stared out the window for a long time, thinking about "matters of consequence" and the responsibility one takes on in the taming of a wild thing. That hit close to home. When Nola Mae got home from school, Jennifer asked if she had ever read it.

"Of course. Hasn't everyone? I have the original version in French if you'd like that."

She listened to Nola Mae's records, and among the newer additions she found some with distinctly Christian words. As she followed along with a Benjamin Britten album, her heart soared in worship, almost to the point of tears, as the richly textured music interpreted and brought to life the ancient words of the "Te Deum."

> We praise Thee, O God,
> We acknowledge Thee to be the Lord.
> All the earth doth worship Thee,
> The Father everlasting.
> To Thee all Angels cry aloud,
> The Heavens and all the Powers therein.
> To Thee Cherubim and Seraphim continually do cry,
> Holy! Holy! Holy! Lord God of Sabaoth!
> Heaven and earth are full of the majesty of Thy Glory.

There were other records, too, in Nola Mae's collection—

oratorios, cantatas, anthems, requiems, masses. Was it all right to listen to Catholic music? she wondered. She didn't know but thought she'd go slow there. A requiem by Brahms seemed different, though. Perhaps she'd try that someday. So much to take in, so much to worship with.

She also did some more assessing of her relationship with Corey, preparing to give him an answer. With sheet of paper in her lap, she set about listing the pros and cons. Corey would like that kind of approach to problem solving, she thought. In the "plus" column she wrote that he was a minister, and she felt her gifts and talents would fit nicely into the role of minister's wife. She liked his looks, though she was careful not to put that at the top of the list. She noted "many things in common," with the mental reserva- tion that there weren't as many as she had originally thought. For instance, she didn't feel free to discuss any of the things she was reading and listening to that were having a profound impact on her life, her spiritual life. She made a notation in the "minus" column.

She admired Corey's ability to deal with people, his or- ganizational and managerial skills, and saw in him a person whom others liked and respected. And he was an excellent preacher—eloquent, dynamic, occasionally spellbinding. Even his judgment texts had served to stir within her a deep feeling of worship, but not necessarily in accord with his particular purposes. He tended to fashion his distinctive texts around his own view of building the church.

Jennifer chewed on the end of her pen after she wrote that, trying to pin down just what disturbed her here. Shouldn't building the church be the greatest good of all? She reflected back on church business meetings, all models of order, efficiency, and productivity. But tentative voices had been raised in some of those meetings that were quickly overridden by Corey's firm leadership. He knew exactly where he wanted the church to go and was not about to bend or yield to what he considered lesser considerations in the name of democracy. It was not that his ideas were bad. The growth and vitality of the Clevis church were witness to that. It was the way he went about it that bothered her. The work was everything—even, she sometimes thought, of more importance than love for God and His people.

Jennifer sighed as she read over her list, discouraged by its ambiguity. But at least Corey was honoring his promise to give her time to think over his proposal.

19 When Jennifer returned to her classroom after three weeks absence, Rosalie was desperately glad to see her. She "talked" a blue streak, and Jennifer's heart ached as she imagined how isolated the little girl had felt in school without any adult who could effectively communicate with her. So she made an effort to spend extra time with the child.

Rosalie's father had just begun tapping out his sugar maples, and she begged Jennifer to drive up to see the operation.

"I carry the spiles," she signed, trying two or three different ways to help Jennifer understand what they were, "and the drill and hammer. My daddy carries the buckets. They're too heavy for me. Tom hauls the buckets up the hill on a sled, but the snow is still deep up in the woods. Daddy says he hopes a lot of it will melt by the time we collect sap. It's so much fun to make syrup. You would like it! Please, *please* come!"

But Jennifer was still recuperating, and the return to teaching took all her energy. In addition, Corey was spending more time with her now, giving her less time to rest. Thus, a couple of weeks went by before she felt up to visiting the Baker farm. She set a date with Rosalie, instructing her to tell her father that she would ride home with Jennifer that day instead of taking the school bus.

The day came, with made-to-order sugaring conditions: a well-below-freezing night followed by a day of bright, warm sunshine. Rosalie was ecstatic and had trouble concentrating through the long school day. But finally dismissal time came, and with much leaping and hopping, the little girl and her teacher set off in Corey's car. "You could've taken my car," said Nola Mae when she heard about it that evening. "Why didn't you ask?"

Jennifer was fully as fascinated by the sugaring operation as Rosalie had predicted. They had quite a climb up through the pasture to the little sugar shack nestled against the woods, but once there, Jennifer had a thousand questions about the procedure.

Orley's face lighted up when the two came into view, and he was more than willing to explain the workings of the small evaporator.

"Y' see, this here front pan gits th' raw sap, an' th' one back by th' chimbley is part b'iled down. Th' pan on this side o' th' middle is where you finish 'er off an' draw off into a bucket an' strain it."

Jennifer looked with awe at the cloud of steam billowing up toward the vents. "It's hard to believe that sap that looks and tastes just like water could turn into such sweet syrup just by cooking it a few hours! How much water do you figure boils off?"

"Wal . . . ," he took off his cap and scratched his head, "it depends. Some years you'll git a thirty-to-one yield, others it's closer t' fifty-to-one. This year I'm thinkin' it's on th' fifty side o' things. A lotta sap, not a gooddeal o' syrup."

113

"It tastes good, though," Jennifer said as she licked off every trace of sweetness from the spoon.

Rosalie led her through the sugar bush along the track that Tom, with a little assistance from Orley's sometime helper Justin had made. Snow was still on all sides, but ever-widening circles around the base of trees and along ruts showed the inroads the warm sun was making upon the cloak of winter, and the tiny rivulets creasing the sunny slope flowed faster as the afternoon wore on.

Orley strained a final batch of syrup from the finishing pan and filled a small jar for Jennifer to take home. "T'ain't much, but it'll sweeten up a mess o' fritters right good. If I hed a bigger jar up here, I'd give y' more." And after seeing that all the pans had sufficient depth of sap in them to prevent their boiling dry and that no live coals remained on the ground that might start a fire, they climbed into the sled behind Tom for the brisk ride down to the barn. Orley and Rosalie urged her to stay for supper, but she declined with genuine regret, having already made arrangements with Corey. She wanted to get back down the mountain before it was pitch dark, so with many expressions of gratitude all around, she took her leave and drove down the shadowy mountain road.

Jennifer truly liked Orley. A hard worker and a good father, he had a warmth and humor about him that more than balanced off the persistent worry lines on his brow.

After crossing the river at Plum, she saw a familiar figure walking along the road toward Clevis, and her pulse quickened. She had heard that Tikki had been in and out of town during the past few weeks, but she had not seen him. She pulled to the side of the road, rolling down her window, and he turned and ambled over.

"Would you like a ride?"

The expression on his face was hard to see in the gathering darkness, but there was no misinterpreting his soft, in-

114

sinuating tone. "Wal, now, that's right friendly. Where would you like t' ride to? Mebbe Charleston, like yer friend and Hizhonor? I ain't pertickaler. Jes' you an' me—won't that give Lover Boy a mite t' think on!"

Panic and dismay throbbed in Jennifer's face. The rumors were true then. Tikki had reverted to his old manner. But why? Why was he acting like this, after nearly killing himself to save her life?

"Tikki, I just don't understand how you can be one person one minute and so different—"

But he cut her off with a torrent so vile that she put her hands over her ears and wept. When he ran down, she tried once again, struggling to keep her voice steady. "I only wanted to say thank you for all you did for me."

"You kin go t' hell with yer thanks!"

"Tikki, I owe you my life!"

"Look, you don't owe me nothin'—I don't owe you nothin'! Th' slate's clean!" He ground the words out. "Now, clear outta here afore I take you up on that ride!"

Jennifer drove away quickly, shaking with fright and dismay. She pulled over again at the edge of town to have her cry before meeting Corey. Actually, when she thought about it, Tikki was behaving with perfect consistency. The only aberration was the episode at her house. She should have been prepared for this. But she wasn't, and it hurt.

For all her care, Corey knew within minutes of her arrival that something was wrong, and she was soon sobbing again in his arms. They talked about it at length, and with commendable restraint he refrained from even implying, "I told you so." He was supportive and constructive, and by the end of the evening she was able to set it aside and think about the better aspects of the day, especially her time with Rosalie and Orley.

Jennifer was not the only person to have instilled in her the fear of Tikki. For about a week Rusty walked about with eyes wide and a certain whiteness around his mouth. When Jennifer questioned him about it, all he would say was that he had been ordered to keep a distance from Tikki of no less than two hundred feet. And having already felt the force of Tikki's capabilities in the skunk episode, Rusty was worried lest he offend without meaning to.

Jennifer saw in this a thread that she might exploit in connection with his friends, Coop and Connie.

"You know, Rusty, if you play around with things and people that you know perfectly well are bad, you're bound to get hurt." (Ouch! That one turned back on herself.) "God has set laws and boundaries, and if we don't pay attention to them because we want freedom, we often find we aren't free at all, only miserable. But God doesn't want us to be miserable. Jesus came to show us how to be really happy with the kind of joy that doesn't depend on the kicks we get out of doing goofy things. Can you see what I'm saying, Rusty?"

His eyes were on the ground, his foot making invisible designs. "Yes'm."

She put her hand under his chin and brought his eyes up to hers. "I want you to go home and read the Twenty-Third Psalm several times, especially the part, 'Yea, though I walk through the valley of the shadow of death, I will fear no evil, for Thou art with me.' Read it until you believe it; then ask God to be with you to keep you out of trouble. Will you do that, Rusty?"

"Yes'm." This time his woebegone eyes clung to hers as to his sole lifeline of hope.

But within another week Rusty was his old self again. Jennifer was pretty sure, however, that fear of Tikki had put into him just a smidgeon of the fear of God.

Spring moved its powerful hand across the earth like a

faith healer, calling forth life and health out of the insentience of winter. Man and beast responded to the quickening rays of the heightened sun with joy and a new devotion to work. Rakes came out, flower bulbs were uncovered, garden soil was studied to see if perhaps a high corner might be dry enough to put in some early peas.

Some of the men of the church had taken on particular chores in an attempt to clean and fix up around the building, so while Ellen tended the store, Randy and Kevin Lindel set off to repair some of the doors before warm weather made them uncloseable. Kevin had drawn a picture of the church that he was anxious to give to Corey, and he found the minister hard at work in his office.

"Why, thank you, Kevin! That's a mighty fine picture!"

And it was fine. The church, positioned in the sky, had its steeple tilted just a bit, and there was an impressive figure in front of the building greeting several smaller people whose arms proceeded from the sides of their heads. Off to the left a tree with a round, black crown towered over a number of tombstones.

"I like that, Kevin. You helping your daddy fix things today?"

The boy nodded, and with a happy smile skipped through the door.

Toward the end of the morning, Randy sent Kevin to ask Corey for help in holding a door in place while he repositioned the hinges. When Corey had gone out to help, Kevin lingered behind to view his gift once again. But it was nowhere in sight—not on the wall where he had hoped to see it, nor on the desk, nor on the floor. He finally found it in the wastebasket. The boy picked it out and gazed at it a long time, then with a faint shrug let it fall back in.

In wintertime, recess duty had been a disagreeable chore.

117

But now that spring was in evidence, Jennifer looked forward to it. She enjoyed walking around the schoolyard, usually with a child or two in hand, drinking in the fragrance of the soft, frost-plowed earth as it emerged from under its dirty and tattered winter quilt.

Two weeks had passed since her encounter with Tikki. She had seen him once or twice at a distance but took care to follow her own advice to Rusty and stayed out of his way. And so on this day, while she was outside with two little girls, she moved to the far side of the school as she sighted Tikki emerging from the woods on the brook trail.

But her heart leapt fearfully when she saw Rosalie run directly across Tikki's path, then trip and fall right in front of him. Jennifer was about to rush like an angry mother hen to Rosalie's rescue when Tikki stopped and gently set the child on her feet, cupping his hands around her face in a tender gesture. Then he went on his way, and Rosalie came skipping back.

Jennifer's heart was still pounding as she met the dancing sprite, so innocent of the danger she might have been in had Tikki been in a less capricious mood. But perhaps he knew Rosalie was deaf and was more inclined toward mercy with her.

"Are you all right?" Jennifer carefully inspected Rosalie's knees and elbows but found nothing more than a couple of surface abrasions.

"Do you know Mr. Granger?" Jennifer asked.

Rosalie looked puzzled, then shook her head after Jennifer repeated the name. She spied Selena Reggis motioning to her and turned away, signing almost to herself, J — drawn with little finger, U — two fingers up, S — closed fist, T — forefinger over thumb, and then forefingers linked enthusiastically together—friend, *good* friend. *Just friend. Well, Rosalie,* mused Jennifer, *you're probably the only person in the whole world who would call Tikki Granger friend—and good friend at that!* The child meandered with slow contentment toward Selena, her ethereal little song blending with the ardent cooing of a mourning dove.

20 The decision to have Rosalie buried from the church was a major victory for both Jennifer and Corey. The funeral director had pushed hard to have the service in Jensen. More convenient all around, he said. Orley would just as soon have had the preacher and Jennifer and one or two other friends come to the house to pray over Rosalie's body and bury her right there on the farm, but Corey explained that interment in a private plot was no longer legal. They both talked to him of Rosalie's love for Jesus and of the church as the appropriate place for her funeral. And so Orley agreed, not out of conviction that it was indeed the right thing, but because in his grief it was easier not to argue.

Jennifer and Corey spent hours ministering to Orley in his small kitchen. Corey was patient while Jennifer and Orley wept, and then he moved on to dealing with Orley's sense of guilt for the carelessness that he saw as responsible for Rosalie's death.

"I seen her a-settin' there under that dead snag puttin' t'gether one o' them dolls o' hern, an' I sez to myself that ain't too safe a place fer her. 'Widder-makers,' they call them things. But 'twouldn't a done no good t' holler, an' my arms was full o' buckets t' put in th' sled. I shoulda set 'em down right then an' gone over t' where she could see me an' got her outta there. But I didn't, an' when I put th' buckets in th' sled, it scared Tom, an' he started up, an' by that time I fergot all about Ros an' th' snag. I was

119

collectin' more buckets when I heard it give way. No wind, no nothin'—it jes' went. An' I coulda saved her!" He held his head in both hands, sobbing.

Any child's funeral is difficult, but this one was especially poignant. Rosalie had been a very special child to many people. The church was nearly full, and this surprised and affected Orley as much as anything in the entire service. He was moved to tears at the sight of all the townsfolk and school children who had come to pay their last respects to his little girl.

The family's friend-of-occasion had not come, which didn't surprise Jennifer when she recalled Orley's remark, "Justin—he don't like t' talk about them things like I do." A helper, perhaps, but definitely not one to give emotional support in time of crisis. He had, however, provided the coffin, a starkly plain but beautifully crafted box.

Jennifer wondered if Tikki might come, since he had performed his small act of kindness for Rosalie just a few days before her death, but he was nowhere to be seen.

Jennifer also felt some apprehension concerning Corey's message, hoping he wouldn't use it as an occasion to berate the townsfolk who never came to church, assailing them with threats of wrath and judgment to come. Or preach to Orley who Corey was convinced didn't understand the way of salvation. But his presentation was unusually gentle and beautiful. The first of the two passages he used was from Matthew, the parable of the two talents. Rosalie, he said had been given less than other children, but had made full use of what she had, not wasting anything in self-pity. And she was now receiving her Master's commendation: "Well done, good and faithful servant! You have been faithful with a few things; I will put you in charge of many things. Come and share your master's happiness!"

The other passage was from Isaiah 55:

> "For my thoughts are not your thoughts,
>   neither are your ways my ways,"
>   declares the Lord. . . .
> "You will go out in joy
>   and be led forth in peace;
> the mountains and hills
>   will burst into song before you,
> and all the trees of the field
>   will clap their hands."

Jennifer was deeply moved as she pictured Rosalie singing and laughing and clapping and *listening* to the music which now surrounded her.

The committal ceremony in the cemetery was especially sad. Orley, small and shrunken under the weight of many years of accumulated suffering, stared through a blur of tears at the small pine coffin with its one bouquet of yellow and white daisies arranged around a hand-made doll. "Ashes to ashes, dust to dust." Was not the sum of his life but a heap of ashes?

Some of the church ladies had prepared refreshments for everyone, but Jennifer needed to be by herself. So after a quick word to Corey, she headed for the pine grove behind her house.

But when she had climbed the slope to the welcoming sanctum, she was startled to see Tikki. He got up quickly at her approach and glowered at her with the full intensity of a gathering thunderstorm. Frightened by his look, she didn't know whether to run or stay. Anyway, she was quite sure she could escape only if he chose to let her. "Tikki—I'm sorry. I didn't know you were up here—"

His face became blotchy, his breathing heavy, and he clenched and unclenched his jaw. Then the explosion came, making him so incoherent that Jennifer at first had difficulty understanding anything he said. But soon she perceived that his wrath centered around Rosalie's death and was aimed at God.

She was dumbfounded. She had observed his gentleness to Rosalie in the schoolyard, but she had had no idea of the depth of his feeling for the child. When he had to stop for breath, she broke in.

"Tikki, God loved Rosalie very much, and—"

But with a furious roar he was on her, sending her sprawling into the duff. *"What kind of a God makes little children deaf an' then kills 'em?"* He turned and flung himself on his knees against a tree trunk and beat on it with his fists. "Oh, *God! God! God!*" His blow had left Jennifer stunned, and she struggled to get a grasp on what was happening and what she should do. After a moment Tikki's sobs broke through her confusion, and with a rush of emotion, she realized the deep hurt that had driven him to hit her. She had come to the grove thinking that, next to Orley, she was the one most affected by Rosalie's death; now she was seeing the searing pain of one who had no hope or consolation, and she wanted to give comfort.

But as she laid a light hand on his shoulder, he wrenched away with a hiss. "Don't touch me—git away!"

She moved back quickly and sat praying in silence. Then she began to speak, softly at first, almost in a whisper.

"Rosalie was truly a special child, and God loved her very much. He gave her extra love and joy, and she was open to the whole world and open to others in a way that very few children—or adults, even—are. I never saw a child who was as gifted in this way, or one who enjoyed life as much as Rosalie did.

"But she had even more. Her mother had taught her about a God who made her and loved her. She told her about Jesus, who came to make her heart pure and clean, but that He Himself had to die in order to do it. Rosalie was so—so very sorry about the suffering that Jesus had to go through, but she somehow understood that He is the source of all that's good in life and the remedy for all that's bad. She didn't look at her deafness as a punishment from God. Anything but! She heard and saw things that ordinary people just pass by, and she knew she did. I'm convinced that God took one thing from her in order to give her a lot more, and she used every bit of what she had been given."

Tikki was lying quietly, and she was encouraged to continue.

"Do you know what Rosalie is doing right now? I can't begin to guess the whole, but at the very least, she's *listening* to Jesus tell her what a splendid, beautiful child she is. *Listening* to music she's never heard before. And she's dancing and clapping and having the time of her life. She *is* alive, Tikki. More alive than the rest of us. It was for this she was made. Death for someone who loves Jesus as Rosalie did isn't the end. It isn't judgment. It's the perfecting and making whole of what this world messes up and wrecks.

"I'll miss Rosalie. I haven't stopped crying since I heard she'd been killed. But it's me I feel sorry for—not her!"

There was still no movement. Jennifer thought a moment and then said, "Tikki, if you would only allow Jesus to—"

But at that he raised up and snarled at her, "Don't give me any of yer spiritual spaghetti!"

Jennifer, startled by the sudden move and sick with disappointment, scrambled to her feet. Her heart torn with fear, compassion, and failure, she turned away from Tikki and wept softly as she descended to the cottage.

The house was empty. Nola Mae had evidently come home after the funeral, left her school things, and then gone out again. Jennifer wandered aimlessly for a while. She wanted so badly to help Tikki, not just to give him comfort, but to lead him to the Comforter. He had come to her for help, she was sure of that. Why else would he have chosen the pine grove in which to do his mourning? He knew she frequented the spot—he knew everything else about her. Her heart ached to be able to reach out to him in some way.

Corey would have written off Tikki's rejection of Jennifer's words as a "hard heart," but she couldn't believe that. Not after hearing those awful sobs. Rosalie had somehow gotten to Tikki in a way no one else had been able to. Jennifer thought once again of that fleeting caress he had given the child in the schoolyard and the happiness it had brought to the little girl's face. With tears, she linked her forefingers in imitation of Rosalie's sign for Tikki—just a friend, but good friend. Rosalie had been everyone's good friend. But now she was dead. No more private finger conversations, no more frail little body leaping into her arms, no more special grass dolls slipped into her school desk drawer.

She wiped her eyes. This wouldn't do; she was becoming maudlin. Her eye fell on a requiem album that Nola Mae had left on top of the stereo, and this reminded her of the one she had been going to listen to. What better time than now?

She searched quickly for the Brahms *Requiem*. Then, text in hand, she settled into her chair and soon shed fresh tears as the music pulled from deep within her the primordial archetypes of Sorrow and Comfort and Triumph.

> Blessed are they that mourn, for they shall have comfort.
>
> Behold, all flesh is as the grass; . . . for lo, the grass withereth and the flower thereof decayeth. . . .Albeit, the Lord's word endureth forevermore!
>
> How lovely is Thy dwelling place, O Lord of Hosts! . . . O blest are they that dwell within thy house: they praise Thy name evermore!
>
> Ye now are sorrowful, but yet ye shall again behold me, and your heart shall be joyful, and your joy no man taketh from you. Yea, I will comfort you, as one whom his own mother comforteth.

Lo, I unfold unto you a mystery. . . . For the trumpet shall sound, and the dead shall be raised incorruptible, and we shall all be changed. . . . For death shall be swallowed in victory! Grave, where is thy triumph? Death, O where is thy sting? Worthy art Thou to be praised, Lord of honor and might.

Caught up in the spiritual intensity of the music, Jennifer was only dimly aware of Nola Mae's return. Nola Mae stopped for a moment just inside the door. Then, setting her package on the floor, she came to the chair, knelt down, and wrapped her arms around Jennifer. The two clung to each other and cried as the music invoked its blessing and comfort.

A blanket of heaviness enfolded Jennifer as she lay in bed that night, the events of the day passing by in a kaleidoscope of confused images. Her whole body ached from the physical and emotional strain.

Corey had been sensitive to her pain and had renewed his proposal, this time with a sympathetic tenderness which drew her to him. She felt hunger within for a place of safety and solace and rest, and for the first time she saw in him the attributes that would provide such a haven. She couldn't possibly make a definite decision on the heels of a day like this, but in a week or two, perhaps after Easter. . . .

21 Spring had come to a full boil in Jennifer's veins. The fragrance that rose from the burgeoning earth seasoned her mélange of sadness, love, and vague yearning for beauty. She longed to go to the mountains across the river, or at least along the trail beside the

river, but she could not—dared not—go alone.

Why, when everything around me is coming to life, do I feel so bound up, so stifled? She wanted to be alive, to explore, to rejoice. Somehow it all had to do with freedom, but she wasn't sure how. She asked Ellen what she thought, and as a result the two friends decided to do their own personal Bible study on the matter.

They elected to do it on a Saturday and enjoy a short bird-watching hike and picnic along with it. Jennifer was delighted to be outside and free from classroom duties that routinely began to pall toward the end of the school year. Ellen enjoyed the break from her household duties and Saturday-with-all-the-kids-home routine.

Neither woman knew many birds beyond cardinals, robins, and blackbirds, but armed with Ellen's old pocket-sized guide with its fuzzy pictures, they started up Maple Avenue and through the cemetery, encouraged by the potpourri of sound all around them.

"There's one!" exclaimed Jennifer. "Sort of gray, smallish, and flops its tail up and down. Right there. See it?"

They studied the bird carefully and then paged through the little book. "A Canada jay, maybe?" offered Jennifer.

"There's just any number of gray birds. We'll never find the right one," moaned Ellen. "Why don't you look for a green bird? There aren't very many of them!"

They did manage to identify a mockingbird that dropped down just ten feet away, but only because Ellen already had an idea of what it was. As they made their way slowly through the schoolyard and the woody patch behind and then on to Hazel Lane, Jennifer ferreted out one bird all on her own, a little downy woodpecker. By the time they reached the pine grove behind Jennifer's place, having first stopped at the house to pick up the picnic basket she had prepared, both women flopped on the needle carpet, exhausted and laughing.

"If only we had a few of those wings we saw," Ellen chuckled. "Our little feathered friends wouldn't be winded by this."

"That's the truth," Jennifer agreed. "For them it's all so effortless, so free. I suppose they run across as many dangers and troubles as any other creature, but somehow birds have always seemed the epitome of freedom to me."

This unplanned comment was a natural lead-in to the study they had intended to do. So as they ate their sandwiches, chips, relishes, and home-made cobbler, they looked at what the Bible had to say about freedom.

First on the list was Romans 8:1 and 2: no condemnation in Christ but freedom from the law of sin and death. Then in close connection, Romans 6:18: freedom from sin but slaves to righteousness. At first this seemed straightforward and encouraging, but with her hidden agenda of personal questions, Jennifer began to wonder if Corey was right after all in his interpretation of what was proper and good for a Christian to do. A slave to righteousness—it sounded terribly forbidding.

Next was James 1:2: obedience to the perfect law that gives freedom.

Ellen was thoughtful as they discussed this. "You know," she finally said, holding out a forkful of cobbler, "there's a right amount of food to eat, but if we are slaves to our appetite, we become bound by the results of it. I wonder if spiritual freedom is like that."

"We're most free when we obey the law of the Spirit, like Romans 8 says." An errant breeze rustled the leaves of Jennifer's Bible, and she searched for the proper page again while Ellen sought to articulate her thoughts further.

"*Most* free? Maybe it's better to say free in the fullest sense of the word. We're not free at all in the eyes of the world, but the quality of our freedom in Christ stands head and shoulders above the quantity of freedom that non-Christians think they have."

Jennifer turned to the Gospel of John. "Look at John 8:31 through 36. Jesus is saying here that if we stick with Him, we'll know the truth, and the truth will set us free. And in verse 34, 'Everyone who sins is a slave to sin.' But we can be free with all the privileges of a son because it's the Son who sets us free."

When they got to the last passage, Colossians 2:8 through 23, things began coming together for Jennifer. It was as though she were standing on a high peak looking in three different directions, trying to decide which way to go. Off to the right stood Corey and his carefully proscribed life built firmly on the rock of the Word. To the left stretched blue, haze-enshrouded mountains that gave rise to mountain men (one in particular), music, flowers, poetry, dancing, singing birds, freedom. In the middle was God, but she could not discern which way He tended, right or left. Was she slave to Christ or free in Christ—or both?

Easter held special meaning this year for Jennifer. Rosalie's death still weighed upon her, but in its light, Jesus' death and resurrection took on a new and specific focus. Two deaths. One like a storm-driven surf crashing against the rocks, the other a tiny pea-pod bark bobbing up and down in a sheltered backwater. The other—because of the One.

"I will not leave you comfortless," Jesus had told His disciples. Had they felt the same sharp stab of pain when in their old, familiar surroundings—everything the same except that He was no longer there? How many times in the past week had Jennifer given instructions to the class and then turned to Rosalie's desk ready to sign to her?

The children missed her, too. Especially her closest companions, Selena and Cindy. Selena in particular had been happy to have Rosalie "mother" her and lead her about in their creative activities. Now at times she would cry quietly at her desk or bury her face in Jennifer's arms.

"I am the resurrection and the life," Jesus said. "The first fruits of them that sleep." Easter always provides many living reminders of life out of death, and this one was especially beautiful, with trees and flowers lending their "Alleluias" to the occasion. The weather had been warm and relatively dry, assuring easy crossing of the Carla for the early morning climb up Sugar Hill.

The Easter Sunrise Service was *the* church event of the year for drawing a crowd. People from Dorsil, Plum, and even a few from Jensen gathered at the ford in the wee chill hours for the trek up the mountain, the way lit only by flashlight. A few came to the west side of the river just to watch the eerie, luminescent line thread its serpentine way through the trees, around the holly sentinel, and on up toward the summit. As soon as the last firefly disappeared from view, the spectators returned to the church to prepare breakfast for the hungry horde.

The star performers headed the parade, and once at the top, they scurried to and fro with much whispering and giggling while the rest of the party heaved themselves up the last steep incline.

According to long custom, the group awaited the actual appearance of the sun in as much silence as they could muster with so large a number. Then, just as it broke the horizon, the teenaged girls sang in slow, soft tones, "Low in the grave He lay, Jesus, my Savior," and the congregation joined with loud, if somewhat tuneless enthusiasm, "Up from the grave He arose—Hallelujah! Christ arose!"

The major offering was a dramatic enactment of the resurrection account as read by Hubie Smith from the Gospel of Mark. To the left of the lookout was a pile of rocks that might, with a bit of imagination, pass for a tomb, and toward this came the three "women" with their baskets of burial spices. The trio—Olivia Reggis and her younger sister Marcella, and Rusty's sister Debbie, all carefully but somewhat insecurely swathed in sheets—emerged from the trees behind the crowd. Marcella was having the most trouble, grabbing at her sliding drapery and trying to hike it back into place, but the battle was lost when the cloth snaked its way to her ankles and left her in an ignominious heap.

Olivia, with a series of extraordinary arm maneuvers, managed to keep her robe intact, but as Hubie intoned, "Who will roll the stone away?" her basket fell, exposing to full view her private cache of chocolate Easter bunnies.

Debbie, grimly clutching both robe and basket, continued doggedly on as Hubie described the women's reaction to the angel at the tomb, "and they were alarmed." Whereupon Rusty, also resplendent in bedsheet, leaped up on the rocks with a horrific yell, and Debbie fled screaming in genuine terror to her mother's arms.

But despite these mishaps, the day went well. The excellent breakfast featured ham and eggs, sour milk cornbread, and Hilda Smith's renowned braided coffee bread. The service was well attended, and afterward Corey took Jennifer to Jensen for dinner. He was in rare form, lavishing charm and attention on her. They walked and talked and joked about the little girls' misfortunes, and Jennifer came into the house feeling truly cared for. The day had been long, having started about four in the morning, but exciting and satisfying to them both.

Tikki showed up the next day for the first time since Rosalie's funeral. Jennifer was coming out of the hardware store when she saw him emerge from Tully's bar and saunter in her direction. He hadn't seen her, she was quite sure. Heart pounding, she debated what to do. She could duck back into the safety of the store, she could walk on home as if she hadn't seen him, or she could wait for him and see what happened. At least she was reasonably safe here in the middle of town.

She decided, instead, on a fourth alternative. Walking quickly past the post office, she turned down the dirt road that led to the river ford and sat on a stump some distance from Main Street and the sidewalk. If he saw her, he would be the one to decide whether or not to talk. She tried to look calm, but her temples beat rapidly.

He passed the post office, saw her, and stopped. Jennifer said nothing but tried to still the quaking within her with a smile of sorts. He stood looking at her for a long moment, then walked toward her.

Jennifer took a deep breath. "Hello. Welcome back."

He studied her, his face a mixture of sadness and suspicion, but with no evidence of hostility. He nodded almost imperceptibly, still watching her closely. Frantically combing her mind for something to say that was both safe and relevant, she borrowed a ploy from one of Nola Mae's books. "If I say it's a nice day, you can make some comment on the unusual weather this spring."

A shadow of a smile played around his mouth, enough to encourage her. She tried a more direct approach.

"Tikki, I've been worried about you. Are you all right?"

Again he searched her face with a guarded expression before answering. "Yes . . . are you?"

"Yes, I am—"

But with another slight nod, he turned and went on his way. Just three words, but it was enough. Her spirits rose, and she sang all the way home.

That night, a plan had its beginnings in her mind. She mulled on it all the next day, Tuesday, veering first for it, then against it, then back again. She knew it was madness, but the adventurer in her led her on. By evening she had decided to carry it through the next day, provided she saw Tikki.

But she didn't. However, the following morning she was surprised to bump into him on her way to school. She saw right away that his basic attitude had not changed since Monday, but she was struck dumb at the unexpected encounter.

"Uh—I was thinking—I would like—I mean—" She could feel her face getting redder by the moment.

"You git caught in th' food grinder this mornin'?"

She laughed nervously. "I'm sorry. I wasn't expecting to see you quite so soon today."

He was watchful but said nothing, so with a big breath she plunged on with her well-rehearsed speech.

"For a long time I've wanted to go to Orley's place by way of the mountain trail, but I know I'd never find the way alone. I'd get lost for sure, and half the town would have to turn out to rescue me a second time, and I'm not sure they mightn't say, 'Good riddance' and just leave me there. But anyway—"

She was talking fast and nervously. Tikki put his hand on her arm. "Whoa! Let's skittle back jest a bit an' scratch out all th' trimmin's. You want t' hike t' Orley's, an' you want me t' tell you how t' git there. That right?"

She blushed. "Well, yes, partly. What I really had in mind was for you to show me the way. Next week is spring vacation and I could go any day. We could start early. I'd make a lunch, and we could eat along the trail somewhere, or I'm sure Orley would be happy to give us something to eat. I've wanted so badly to walk the woods and hills and see all the laurel and spring flowers." She finished in a rush of words, braced for the smirk to spread over his face, but Tikki showed only a quizzical look of surprise.

132

"Hit's over four miles t' Orley's, an' I reckon you'd git yer fill o' woods an' hills afore we was home agin. You sure you know what kinda tree 'tis y're barkin' 'round? Seems t' me y're aimin' t' hev lunch in th' lions' den."

"Well," she smiled, "I figure if I can get the lion to protect me, I'll be safe enough. And besides, you saved my life, and so I trust you. Will you do it, Tikki?"

He stood a moment gazing beyond her, then said he would. They planned to meet at the ford on Tuesday if it wasn't raining, and Jennifer volunteered to bring a lunch.

Just before they parted, Tikki once more looked searchingly into her face. "You sure you know what you're about?"

Her eyes widened, and she answered solemnly. "Tikki, I *trust* you." With a satisfied nod, he went on his way.

The rest of the day went by for Jennifer in a blur of excitement. But as the week drew to a close, her anticipation was tempered by apprehension and guilt over the clandestine aspects of the outing. She wondered what to tell Corey. She wasn't about to lie to him, so she solved the problem, at least temporarily, by saying nothing at all.

22   Jennifer crept out of bed in the early morning gloom. Light showed in the sky out across the river, but the hills were a blockade fighting to hold night close to the ground. She tried to be very quiet but was nervous and therefore clumsy. By the time she had gotten herself ready and the lunch packed, she had stumbled over a chair, knocked the thermos lid on the floor, and stepped on the cat. When she eased open the front door, her teeth were chattering with excitement.

Light had finally overcome. The early chorus of birdsong had passed, but down by the river a wren poured forth his bubbling cascade from a scraggle of honeysuckle. Raskolnikov had come out with Jennier, and a mockingbird heralded his presence with a loud "Cat! Cat!"

Get ahold of yourself, Jen! she told herself. *After all, you're just going for a hike to Orley's.* But it didn't work. She knew this was not just a hike but a secret outing with a potentially dangerous man. And she was more than a little afraid. Her instinct told her it would be all right, but her mind paraded before her all the obscene things Tikki had said to her in the past. She was gambling, she knew, betting heavily on the deep vein of gentleness she had seen more than once. She thought of Corey and looked about furtively as though expecting to see him come around the corner.

The sun had risen, but not on Clevis. It would be another hour before the hills surrendered to its rays. Until then, the morning mists would cling in pockets up the greening hillsides like gossamer clouds resting till the sun signaled them to return to the sky.

Her heart thumped wildly as she turned down River Street onto the dirt track leading to the ford. She hoped desperately that Tikki was there waiting for her, and equally desperately that she was early and could calm herself a bit. When she reached the steep slope and didn't see him, her mind gave a leap, then leapt the other way when she spied him downstream, crouched by the edge of the water. He stood and smiled when he saw her make her way down the loose shale bank, and Jennifer knew in an instant that she had won her gamble.

He took the canvas bag from her. "What y' got in here?"

"Some lunch. And a loaf of bread for Orley."

"Think it'll make it thet fur?" he grinned. He felt through the cloth. "Pretty solid lunch there. That th' sandwiches or th' bread?"

"That's the thermos!"

"Thermos! Whad d'we need a thermos fer? They's a hunnert springs an' brooks where we're a-goin', an' we sure don't need t' lug along a thermos. Tell you what. We'll jes' hev a little drink now, an' then stash it acrost th' river till we git back. Unless you jes' have t' hev it, in which case, you'll be obliged t' carry it."

Jennifer's heart sang. Tikki was in good humor. And he was clean! The braid-trimmed leather shirt, as much a part of him as his skin, had undergone quite a transformation. Though not spotless, it was several shades lighter and quite acceptable. His hair and beard, while still strangers to a comb, were likewise clean, and his whole appearance was of disciplined wildness and strength. Joy bubbled within her like the wren's song as he led the way over the big flat stones.

That this docile stream could at times be a raging monster was hard to imagine now. During one rainy spell, Jennifer had stood above the gorge listening to rocks grinding and bumping along in the torrent. Sometimes even the boulders that made up the ford were moved downstream and had to be hauled back by Virgil Hanover's mules.

The walk along the gorge where she had had her first encounter with Tikki was beautiful almost beyond bearing. The hemlocks down below were dark splotches against the pale green wash of the new-leafed trees. Slanting rays of sun pierced the patchy mist over the river and touched the opposite bank with silver and gold. Neither of them spoke as they walked through curtain after curtain of shimmering light, the cool air from the gorge clinging to shady patches and laden with smells of wet rocks and moss and winter-flattened leaves.

They climbed until they reached a narrow track that led to the edge of the gorge. Tikki took Jennifer's hand, and in a few moments they came out several hundred feet above the river at a point roughly opposite her house. They were up high enough to see the sunlit roof and back corner of her home below the pine grove. Also visible were the other houses on Hazel Lane, the church and back section of the cemetery, the gravel pit on Laurel Road, and even Galina Kostyukov's small cottage on the west edge of town. Ever-rising courses of hills surrounded the whole, with the Cricket Knob and Foar's Knob range ahead and to their left, and Sugar Hill behind them to their right.

Jennifer shivered as she peered down at the white water cascading through the narrow ravine. The ground just in front of them fell off sharply in rocky shale. Here and there a tree hung upended from the upper rim of the gorge, its rotted remains a relic of wind and weather. Across from them the bank was lower and not so steep, with dark trees and rhododendrons hunkered down almost to the water's edge, and horizontal planes of dogwood etched against the green backdrop. She could have stayed much longer, drinking in the view, the sharp morning air, and the sound of the river, but Tikki pulled her around without a word, and they went back out to the main trail.

A few hundred feet further, the path began to bear left and then crossed a brook, heading due north alongside the brook and away from the river. They climbed in earnest now, and Jennifer was quickly out of breath. She tried to keep stride with Tikki, who was breathing only slightly harder than normal, but when he turned to see how she fared, she was red-faced and wheezing. He stopped immediately.

"You tryin' t' do yerself in so I'll hev t' haul y' out?"

"I guess I'm more out of shape than I thought," she gasped, laughing sheepishly.

With a look of concern, he led her to the base of a big hickory tree and left her sitting while he went to the brook to wet a large blue handkerchief for her to wipe her face.

"We still got a fur piece t' go, but you'll never make it this way 'less y' pace yerself. I shoulda knowed you'd be blowin' pretty hard an' gone slower. I'm sorry."

Jennifer leaned back against the rough bark, eyes closed, soaking in the attention. Had Corey ever said, "I'm sorry?" She guessed he had when it was something trivial, but she couldn't remember a real apology. She was more and more impressed with this mountain man. Tikki seemed to have an innate gentleness and gentility beyond that of many men she knew.

As they went on at a more sedate pace, her estimation of him rose even more. Perfectly at home and at ease in the woods, he was on speaking terms with specific trees, and recognized birds by their song or even a single call note. Frequently he led her off the trail to inspect some aspect of forest life such as a trillium or a patch of blood-root. They chewed on wintergreen leaves and berries. They crushed and smelled mint leaves. There wasn't anything Jennifer asked that he didn't know about, including its name. Where had she heard that to be able to name something was to have it in your power? If that was true, Tikki had enormous power here in the mountains.

They left the brook and made their way over a low ridge and then down to another valley, crossing over a treacherous stretch of ravine. Higher up now and turning eastward back toward the brook, they moved out of the woods into a hemlock grove. The trees were tall and straight with thick trunks and a carpet of fine needles underneath. Jennifer felt as though she had stepped into a vaulted cathedral. They stood silent, looking up into the dark green canopy and listening to the flute tones of a nearby wood thrush.

"It's so beautiful, it almost makes me cry!"

Tikki smiled and put his arm around her shoulder.

"It even smells different," she said.

He nodded. "They ain't very many groves this big in these mountins, and it's kinda too bad the trail goes through this one. Somebody'll git chainsaw-happy one o' these days."

He picked up the cloth bag. "They's a spot near here thet's good fer lunchin'. We kin hev a sanwich t' keep us movin' along up Plaggett."

He led her to a shelf of ground about ten feet above the brook. The great hemlocks spread out their knobby roots over the rocky ledge, and mosses of assorted shadings and textures crept up to meet the soft, spongy carpet.

Jennifer exclaimed with delight and sat down to look at the brook.

"Whoa! Afore y' git too comf'table, I'd like fer us t' go look at somethin'. We kin leave th' lunch here." Tikki pulled her up and helped her down the bank and across the brook. They were soon out of the hemlocks, but Tikki said, "We'll hit 'em agin up ahead, an' when we do, don't make no noise. Tiptoe, an' don't talk. Watch fer sticks that might crack."

They crept along, getting close to a small, deep glen. A bit further along, Tikki pulled her down, and they crawled, Jennifer trying hard to be as silent as he was. Slowly they maneuvered their way to the edge, and Jennifer peered down. With a combination of pointing and sign language, Tikki directed her eyes to a grassy patch behind some low shrubs. There, the mottled sunshine camouflaging it almost beyond perception, lay a doe, and close by her side a very small spotted fawn.

Jennifer gripped Tikki's hand till her fingers ached. With the only sound around them the strident tones of a bird proclaiming its territory, they lay silent for several minutes, then backed slowly away and returned to the open woods.

But before they'd gone far, Tikki stopped. Two small brown birds with silver-streaked breasts were pacing and flitting, clucking in alarm. Tikki began talking softly to them. "You got a nest hereabouts, don't you? Wondered why you was makin' sech a racket." He walked around carefully, signaling Jennifer to stand still. Soon he bent over and motioned to her. There on the ground was a small domed nest with four mottled eggs inside.

"Ovenbird," Tikki pronounced, and Jennifer wondered where she'd been all her life to know so little.

A little way further, Jennifer spotted some hair and bones. Tikki told her it was the remains of a small deer that had probably starved to death during the winter.

"Then it wasn't killed by another animal?"

"May've been. But I hev seen 'em drop without a mark on 'em—usually runty ones." Seeing her distressed look, he said, "Them that dies feeds flies an' worms an' beetles an' other animals, an' they break it down so plants kin feed, and finally another deer comes along fer his breakfast. Each critter's got his own special job, what he's made t' do, an' he does it without much fuss 'r worry."

Back at the ledge, Jennifer chewed on what Tikki had said as she ate her sandwich. Ellen had told her pretty much the same thing: Jennifer had been designed to fill a specific niche in her world. Her job was not the same as Corey's, nor his the same as hers. He was good at preaching and witnessing, she was good at teaching—and learning, maybe? She should find her contentment in doing what she did best and not worry too much about expectations other people had of her.

She watched with satisfaction as Tikki finished a piece of her apple cake and leaned back against his hemlock with a sigh of contentment. She could scarcely believe she was sitting here with this mountain man who had tormented her so much all year. What was more, she felt totally at ease with him. He was being friendly, affectionate even, but there was a well-defined line over which he never stepped to take advantage of her vulnerability. She realized now that her gamble had been on more than just how cordial he would be. Being here in the mountains, so far removed from the security of other people, frightened her for an instant, but nevertheless she felt safe here with Tikki. And free.

Now and then, especially when Corey came into her thoughts, the guilt she had been suppressing made her feel uneasy. It wasn't just that her relationship with Corey was understood by everyone—Corey included—to be more than it actually was. How would she explain if suddenly they were to meet some church people on the trail? How could she explain to God? Somehow she felt the latter to be less formidable than the church folk.

But she couldn't escape the fact that she had wanted this walk with Tikki, wanted it to the extent of closing her mind to what God might want. *I fled Him down the labyrinthine ways/ of my own mind. . . . For, though I knew His love Who followèd,/ Yet was I sore adread/ Lest, having Him, I must have naught beside.* Sooner or later, this little adventure would have to be brought before God. But not now. . . .

Now there were other things to think of, something even deeper, and she wasn't sure she could put her finger on it. It had to do with her growing rebelliousness toward some things that were part and parcel of Corey's personality. Was it his personality? Or was it his beliefs? Perhaps it was the essence of Corey—she didn't know. His mother loomed large in the picture, but Jennifer had made a genuine effort to keep her feelings for the two individuals separate. But how successful had she been? And was it only wishful thinking to hope that Corey was not like his mother? Maybe he could not possibly be otherwise.

One thing she did know. Out here with Tikki she felt a freedom she had never experienced with Corey. She had room to breathe and saw herself as Jennifer. With Corey she felt boxed in. It always seemed that to disagree with him was tantamount to disagreeing with God. Trying to explain how she felt about witnessing or movies would most certainly bring on his patient disapproval—better, perhaps, than a direct put-down, but more demoralizing and demeaning in its effect. She could never really talk about problems with Corey. He was always right, and her ideas counted for little except to be politely listened to and then just as politely demolished. Already with Tikki, she sensed that it would be different.

She stared down at the water striders rowing aimlessly on the smooth surface of the brook. She saw reflected the feathery hemlock branches and patches of blue sky with a small fleecy cloud balanced on one of the boughs. *Waters ripple and flow, slowly passes each—* Suddenly she discovered that by changing the focus of her eyes slightly she could see first the surface reflection and then the brown pebbly stream bed, back and forth. Just a very slight muscle adjustment brought a totally different perspective. Almost like two completely different objects . . .

Tikki broke into her reverie by standing up. "We still got more'n an hour's hike ahead of us, so we'd best be a-truckin' along. We've a'ready done more sightseein' than we shoulda, an' our time with Orley's gittin' shaved down more'n he'll want." He smiled as he pulled her to her feet. "You still able t' walk? Don't want t' turn back?"

"Of course not! I'm fine."

"Now, we kin go one o' two ways. Th' main trail goes out around th' knob an' ain't so steep, but's it's quite some longer. The other goes up over th' shoulder an' cuts off mebbe a mile, but y' got th' climb. Which're y' up fer?"

"Which is prettiest?"

"Well, it's six a one, half a dozen the other. Y' do git a view in a couple a places goin' up over, but then they's a pretty nice waterfall goin' t'other way."

"Let's go up over now and come back the other way."

He grinned. "Was hopin' you'd say that. They's a spring orchid I wanted t' show you way up th' shoulder. Hit's got no business bein' up so high, but it's there in a little marshy dip, an' prob'ly no one else in th' whole world knows about it 'cept us."

Jennifer would have missed this mountain trail if she had been alone. Tikki explained that he took considerable pains keeping the cutoff invisible. A perfectly good trail went up from the road to the fire tower, so the fewer folks who knew about this one the better, in his opinion.

This track differed markedly from the smooth pathway they had just left, and it was steep, rough, and hard to follow unless you were Tikki. He led the way, helping her over difficult places.

They stopped to rest partway up, sitting on a fallen tree. As Jennifer caught her breath, she looked around and noticed the difference in the leaves at this elevation. The maples were just beginning to show lacy green, the brown "horns" on the beeches were just unfolding, and the hickories were still tightly closed. Here there was only an occasional evergreen, and rhododendron was being replaced by mountain laurel.

"They must be beautiful when they're in bloom," she sighed.

"Uh-huh." He was clearly not paying attention. He was looking all around, sniffing the air.

"What is it?" Jennifer asked.

He didn't reply but went on up the hill in great strides, halting again on a small plateau. Jennifer puffed along behind him the best she could, glad for each time he stopped. They weren't far from the top of the mountain, and now even Jennifer could sense something alien to the spring air.

"What is it?" she repeated.

"Fire. An' I don't know where it's comin' from!"

23 *If a person dies on top of a mountain, does it take less time to get to heaven?* Jennifer wondered. *If he doesn't slow down, my heart is going to burst!*

She was being half dragged, half carried toward the summit, and Tikki himself was breathing heavily. Once she suggested he go on without her, but he wouldn't hear of it.

When the grade began leveling off and the trees diminished to shrub-like cover, Tikki let her pause for breath and went on ahead. "Take yer time, but I may need you t'fetch me a rock if I cain't git th' lock open."

Jennifer moved along slowly, but almost immediately she heard the heavy clang of Tikki's feet on the metal stairway of the tower. When she came around the last bend in the path, the square, glass-windowed box on legs of steel rose before her. It was about forty feet high, set on concrete piers that were securely bolted to the bedrock, and the whole structure further anchored by cables on every side.

When she reached the base, Jennifer could see that Tikki had somehow managed to open the door at the top, but a provoked "Damn!" indicated another snag. She was about to start climbing the staircase when he leaned over the railing. "See if you kin find a rock—small enough t' carry easy but big enough t' hev some heft." Loose stones of that size were scarce on the weather-scoured mountain top, but she finally located one and had started up the first of the three tiers of steps when he called down, "Nev' mind. I got it."

As she reached the third tier, her attention was riveted by Tikki's voice. She stopped dead in her tracks, feet on two

143

different treads, wondering if she were hallucinating. She heard Tikki speaking, giving out detailed information: the tower from which he was calling, the location of the fire, wind direction and velocity, and the probable extent and nature of the fire. It was his voice—but it wasn't Tikki. The report being given was articulate and totally devoid of mountain dialect.

She broke through her paralysis and continued on up into the little square room. Tikki was leaning over a table on which there was a large topographic map and a sighting instrument of some kind; in one hand he held a radio transmitter, while with the other he ran his finger down an instruction manual as though making sure he hadn't forgotten anything. He signed off and switched over for a reply; but when the voice on the other end requested his identity, he shut down the unit and quickly stowed it back in its wooden cabinet, clicking shut the padlock he had somehow opened.

Drawing a deep breath, he seemed irresolute, as though unsure of how to proceed. Then he roused himself and turned to Jennifer and said, "It's at Orley's, and we got to get to him as quick as possible. He's scared t' death of fire. Probably that dry pine slash."

Jennifer's mind had been so busy with this new turn of events that it hadn't even occurred to her to look out at the magnificent panorama and the wispy trail of smoke that was wafting over the shoulder of the mountain.

Tikki flashed a quick smile at her. "Are you ready for another wild run? At least this time it's downhill all the way."

He picked up the lunch bag, and they went out onto the walkway surrounding the tower room. Tikki locked the door, and they climbed down to begin the sharp descent to the road.

The first part was treacherous, but further down, the trail

changed from rocks to well-trod dirt, and the going was much easier. They had run nearly the whole way, when Tikki stopped suddenly, almost taking Jennifer's arm off. Then she heard it, too—voices and laughter up the road, near Orley's woodlot. The tinder-dry pine slash left after his fall logging had evidently gone up in a spectacular blaze and burned out just as quickly, but there was an audience to the conflagration. Tikki's face turned hard as steel.

"Damn kids! I'll kill 'em!" He started off but then turned back to Jennifer. "Cross over into them trees an' stay outta sight. Wait there for me." And he took off at a run.

Jennifer was certain she recognized Coop's explosive laughter, and she assumed Connie was with him. But was Rusty there, too? Perhaps they hadn't set the fire, though, and had just happened by. Would Tikki wait long enough to find out?

She listened tensely, expecting an explosion any moment, but was surprised to hear murmurs of calm, even jovial conversation. Tikki's stock rose another notch in her eyes. Evidently he was not in the habit of leaping in and meting out justice, needed or not. With a sigh of relief, she was looking around for a tree to settle against to rest her aching, trembling legs when sounds of mayhem erupted up the road. Shouts and cries and cussing mingled with dreadful thwacking noises. She put her hands over her ears to block out the sound. Why was it so terrible to hear in real life what would not turn a hair if viewed on television?

After what seemed an eternity, the din subsided, and Tikki came jogging back toward her. He was breathing heavily, his eyes still flashing thunder and lightning. "Let's go find Orley. Up this way." He led her through the trees.

"Was it Coop and Connie?" she asked.

"Yep."

She hesitated. "And Rusty?"

"Nope."

Thank you, Lord! She was able to breathe again. The other two boys deserved every bit of what they got, but Rusty wasn't mean—just easily influenced.

"You're bleeding."

"So are they!" He looked grim and forbidding, and she thought it prudent to keep quiet.

He pulled her along rapidly until they reached one of Orley's skid trails that quickly brought them to the lower pasture. Tikki stopped and hollered through cupped hands, but there was no answer. They hurried through the pasture toward the barn, Tikki calling out from time to time. Jennifer was frightened. She remembered Orley describing the mine fire and his subsequent fears. And there was Tikki, too. How would he react if something had happened to Orley? She didn't know how well-acquainted he was with the farmer, but obviously he knew something about him. Would another catastrophe put him all the way back to the abyss of the pine grove? *Lord, please let Orley be all right!* she prayed.

They found him on the ground behind the chicken house, the door of the coop unlatched so the birds could escape the flames that never came. He was alive but blue and obviously in much pain. His eyes lit up as Jennifer and Tikki knelt beside him. With his gaze locked on Tikki's face, Orley's fingers spelled out J - U - S - T and a crooked forefinger. In response, Tikki encircled Orley's finger with his own and, laying his head on the little man's chest, wept.

Nola Mae's vacation week was not going according to her blueprint. The plan had been to stay with a friend in Charleston, play golf with Jeremy, and finish off the week at a folk festival near Pipestem. But due to an emergency, her friend couldn't have her, the folk singer she and Jeremy had most wanted to hear cancelled out, and, worst of all, Jeremy pleaded school responsibilities to renege on the golf. The latter made her uneasy. Some time ago, one of her more frank acquaintances had hinted that Nola Mae's days as top cookie were numbered. Someone new had come on the scene with sufficient flash and style to pose a serious threat to the no-less-attractive but now commonplace Nola Mae, and Jeremy Thurston Tybolt was easily bored. He hadn't come right out and said anything yet, but things were definitely not right. So after a fruitless couple of days trying to work out an alternate arrangement, she came home Monday night in somewhat less than good humor. Thus, she slept late Tuesday morning, until Hilda Smith came looking for Jennifer around eleven o'clock.

"She's an early riser, ain't she? Saw her go by my house afore sunup an' thought she might be back by now."

"That makes two early risers on the street, doesn't it?" replied Nola Mae. "And she, at least, was tending to her own affairs."

Hilda huffed a bit, but when no information was forthcoming from Nola Mae, she went back down the street to Ellen Lindel's.

"No, I haven't seen her. Have you tried Corey? If I do see her, I'll tell her you're looking for her, Hilda," Ellen said.

Corey had no knowledge of her whereabouts either and was a bit put out because he had hoped to do some curriculum planning with Jennifer for Vacation Bible School. "She must have borrowed Nola Mae's car to go to Jensen."

"No. Nola Mae's car's right in th' driveway. I saw it. She must be in town somewhere. I'll just keep lookin'."

"What was it you wanted her for?" Corey asked.

"Oh, nothin' much. I, uh—" Hilda hadn't thought to arm herself with a plausible reason for her inquiries, but she felt her concern was justified. If something untoward had befallen the girl, she just might be a key witness.

A further check around town turned up no new clues, so she went unsatisfied into the store to relieve Hubert for a few hours.

With a "witchity, witchity, witchity," a yellow-throat staked its claim among the cloud-like shad bushes along the edge of the wood. A large hawk circled overhead, soaring on thermals that rose from the warm clearing. A steer lowed beseechingly from the upper pasture, and several hens clucked comfortably around the tableau on the grass.

"Orley, we got t' git you to a hospital," Tikki said.

But the stricken man shook his head. "'Tain't no use," he whispered. "Jes' leave me lay here. A man cain't ask fer more'n t' hev his two best friends by his side t' send 'im off. Justin, you'll take keer o' my animals, won't you? That were a concern. Didn't know how long 'fore anybody'd take notice."

Tikki nodded and gently wiped the beads of perspiration from his friend's ashen face.

"Can I get you a glass of water?" Jennifer asked.

Again Orley shook his head. "All's I want is t' go an' be with Sara and Rosalie." He looked pleadingly into Jennifer's eyes.

She drew a deep breath. "Orley, both Sara and Rosalie loved Jesus very much. Do you love and trust Him?"

"I ain't as good as they was." He coughed painfully.

148

Tikki raised his shoulders and cradled him in his arms.

Jennifer was trembling with nervousness. "It doesn't matter how good or bad you are, Orley, it's how much you believe and trust in Jesus that counts." She tried to think of an illustration he could relate to. "It's like when you go out logging. You couldn't haul those logs out alone, no matter how hard you tried, but with Tom to pull them for you, you get the job done. It's like that with Jesus. He lived a life that *was* good enough, and—"

"He's gone," Tikki said.

No! How can he be? Please, Lord, let him be with Sara and Rosalie! Jennifer covered her face with her hands and cried.

She thought of Tikki and looked up quickly. His face was white, his jaws clenched, but he was otherwise composed.

They sat in silence for several minutes, then Tikki carried Orley's body into the house and laid it on his bed. As he straightened, they heard the fire truck coming up the drive. Tikki put his hand on Jennifer's arm. "Stay in here, out of sight. After they leave, I'll check the animals and we'll go along. I'll arrange tonight t' have 'em taken care of."

"What about Orley? We can't just leave him here!"

"Why not? He's not here. He's with Sara and Ros," he said with a wry grin. "I'll take care of it."

He was back in less than an hour, having talked with the men and fed the animals. He insisted that he and Jennifer eat their lunch, though neither felt hungry. "The way this day is going, we may wish we had twice as much t' keep us fortified."

They returned by way of the lower, longer trail around Plaggett Knob. Around them the trees rang with caroling birds, and the whole earth seemed vibrant, poised for the fruitful season ahead.

But this was lost on the two walkers. Jennifer, her mind awhirl with new and unfathomable information, held each piece up to the old data, but nothing made sense. Tikki—Justin; third-grade reading level—perhaps as well educated as she. *Who? What? Why?*

She tried to question him when they stopped to rest, but he gently cut her off. "Don't even ask. I won't tell you . . . not now, anyway."

"But sometime?"

His eyes, sad and pensive, gazed off into the trees. He didn't answer for a long time, seeming to measure the dimensions of the melancholy within him to see if it could ever fit into words. Finally, he turned with a smile and put his arm around her shoulder. "Sometime . . . maybe. Can you live with that—for my sake?"

Tears came to her eyes, but she smiled and nodded. "Yes. I will."

They talked little the rest of the way, except for Tikki asking her not to report Orley's death.

As they began the last descent on the trail that led to the river, a nameless fear grew within Jennifer. She wanted to stop Tikki, persuade him to turn back with her—where, she didn't know. She only knew she didn't want to leave him or the woods, didn't want to cross the river and re-enter her cage. But, even worse, the conviction grew that inside the cage were furtive, shadowy figures stalking her, ready to pounce when least expected. She clung tightly to Tikki's hand.

But when they turned onto the gorge trail, he stopped and set down the lunch bag. "This is as far as I'll go with you. Too many people over there with telescopes to keep their tongues busy. I won't be far away till you get across the river, so if you need help, just holler."

She looked up at him and whispered. "I don't want to go back."

His face bore evidence of his own conflict, but with almost visible resolve, he stiffened himself for the ordeal at hand. With a deep breath, he began.

"There are a couple of things I need to tell you. First, I want you to promise you won't tell *anyone* you've been with me today." He smiled. "I'm assuming you didn't already tell Corey."

She shook her head. "I didn't tell anyone."

"Good. I don't know how you're going to do it, but it's important that you not let your name get mixed up with mine in today's doings. There's going to be trouble, and I don't want you hurt by it. Will you promise me?"

Her eyes widened, the vague, stalking forms suddenly taking shape. "What kind of trouble? What will happen? Please, Tikki! Please stay out of town!"

"I plan to, but it won't make any difference. There'll be a big flap, whether I'm there or not. You can count on it." He was silent a moment, and with her forefinger she traced along the jagged scar on his thumb. With another deep breath he went on. "And number two, I'm going away. I can't tell you where or why, but I am going. It's the right time." His words were as gentle as he could make them.

Another of the shadowy figures rose out of the mystic vapor of her mind. "But you'll be back in a couple of weeks," she said.

He shook his head. "No."

"When? You will be back sometime?" Panic was invading her voice.

"Maybe sometime, maybe never. Don't count on it. This is the way it has to be. Can you live with that, too—for my sake?"

She was crying, shaking her head dismally. "No! No! Please don't go!"

His expression heavy with sorrow, pain, and compassion, he cupped his hands around her face, and with a light kiss on her forehead, he was gone.

Jennifer sank down and wept for some time, unable to bear this last blow. But she knew he would be watching up river for

151

her to cross. She wanted to wait there, to make him come back to her, but "for his sake" thought better of it. Finally, she went on down the trail.

At the ford she stood a moment watching the flakes of gold disappear from the surface of the water as the sun settled behind the hills. "Waters ripple—"

No, wrong verse.

> Dear one, well dost thou know
>   Why fond lovers must part;
> Wherefore falters thy faith?
>   Why so timid thy heart?
>
> Dearest lover come back;
>   End the vigil I keep.
> Thine, the key to my heart,
>   Mine, without thee to weep!

She was crying again as she made her way across the ford, and about halfway over she heard the splash of a stone upstream. She stopped and strained to see Tikki once more, but he was nowhere visible. She went on across, and the bars of her cage clanged shut behind her.

"My land, child, where've you been? Everyone's been worried half t' death about you, an' Corey called—"

Tikki was right about the telescopes. "I'm sorry, Hilda, but I'm very tired and can't talk now. Good night."

 **25** Rusty was the first to acquaint Jennifer with the village gossip and brewing storm.

When she arrived home from her long day with Tikki,

she fell into bed and slept like one dead. In the morning, Nola Mae got up early and was about to leave for a confrontation with Jeremy when she heard frantic pounding at the door. It was a wide-eyed Rusty.

"Where's Jennifer?" he demanded.

"She's in bed—sleeping."

"I gotta talk to her."

"Well, you can't. Come back later," Nola Mae snapped.

"But I *gotta*. You don't know!"

"No, you don't *gotta*. As long as it isn't the house burning down, whatever you have to tell her can wait till she wakes up."

They stood at an impasse, Nola Mae adamant and Rusty shifting about nervously, trying to think of a different angle, until they heard muffled sounds from Jennifer's bedroom. With a look of disgust, Nola Mae let him in and absolved herself of further responsibility by leaving.

Jennifer emerged from her room, sleepy, tousled, and tying her robe. But one look at Rusty and she was immediately awake. "What is it?"

"It's Tikki, ma'am. He's gone an' done a turrible thing this time! He set fire t' Orley Baker's woodlot an' killed Orley an' beat up Coop an' Connie when they tried t' stop 'im!"

Jennifer sat down and put a hand to her face. So that was the shape of things! The boys had twisted their own mischief and laid it on Tikki. But who would believe them? Surely anyone acquainted with them would know they were lying.

With a sinking feeling, she remembered her promise to Tikki. How easy it would be to say, "He didn't do it. I was with him all day. This is what really happened." But she had promised.

"Rusty, did you talk with Connie and Coop yourself? Isn't it possible that they're lying?"

"Yes'm, I talked with 'em, an' they ain't lyin'! I know that! Connie had a tooth knocked out an' both of 'em look like they was punchin' bags! They ain't lyin'!"

"No, I don't mean about being beat up. I mean about who set the fire. Don't you think that's the kind of prank they might think up, and maybe Tikki caught them, instead of the other way around?"

"No, it couldn't be. If they'd a set th' fire an' said it was Tikki done it, they'd know f'r sure he'd catch up with 'em. I wouldn't sleep another wink if 'twas me done sech a thing!"

Jennifer was silent. This wasn't going to be easy. If she couldn't convince Rusty, who knew the boys and Tikki so well, how could she hope to convince anyone else?

Toward evening, she became afraid for Tikki's life, having heard talk of a posse being formed to hunt him down, or if this couldn't get official sanction, vigilantes rising up. Most unsettling were the local hotheads who could collect a following from other towns and carry out their vendetta, especially with a little alcohol to help them. Coop's father, Matt Cooper, was angriest of these, but there were others as well.

In tears, she went down Sycamore Road to Ray Windle's bungalow near the river. He was eating a late supper in preparation for what he suspected might be a long night. He came out on the porch and listened as Jennifer, with shaking voice, expressed her concern for Tikki. She got as far as her conviction that Tikki was innocent and began to cry.

"Oh, Ray, I know he didn't do it because I was there! He made me promise not to tell anyone I was with him . . . so I wouldn't be mixed up in the trouble he knew was coming. But I can't just keep quiet and let him be killed!"

Ray asked her to give him the whole story. Jennifer told him about their walk to Orley's and the gallop up to the fire tower—leaving out Tikki's altered speech and mentioning only that he didn't want to say who was giving the report. Ray nodded, and she went on to describe their descent to the road, Coop and Connie's joking and laughter, and their comeuppance at Tikki's hands. She said she thought Tikki had used some sort of trick to get them to admit their guilt before laying into them. Again he nodded.

She told of Orley's fear of fire and of Tikki's anxiety to get to him. And she described Orley's last moments, omitting all reference to Justin. "He said not to report the death, that he would take care of everything."

"Mmm." Ray moved over to the porch railing and sat down to ponder what she had told him. After a moment he said, "I talked to the fire warden this morning, and he said he'd spoken to Tikki yesterday at Orley's. They'd gotten the call an' gone up with a truck, but th' fire was out by th' time they got there. Said Tikki didn't have much t' say. He didn't know where Orley was—probably in town, and since th' fire hadn't spread or done much damage once th' slash burned up, they left. The warden thought I oughta know that Tikki was there, especially when he heard Orley was dead. But now what you say puts a whole 'nother light on things." He rubbed his chin thoughtfully. "You were there when the forest unit came?"

"I was in the house when Tikki talked with them. We had just gotten Orley inside. He told me to stay out of sight. His concern for me is just making a big mess for him!"

Ray scratched his head, drew a breath, and looked perplexed. "How long were you there after that?"

"We left after Tikki fed the animals, and came back by the lower trail. He wouldn't come across the river . . . he didn't want anyone to see us together."

"And you don't know where he went or what he did after that?"

"No. He just said he'd take care of Orley and see to the animals."

Ray nodded, as though that fit in with some of his own scanty information. "Well, evidently he got ahold of one of Orley's friends, a guy who gives him a hand once in a while, and—"

"Justin?" She was having trouble with her voice again.

Ray raised his eyebrows, and Jennifer wondered if she'd said too much.

"Yeah, Justin," Ray continued. "He's the one who contacted th' funeral home and plunked down money and a casket. He told them to bury Orley next to his wife and daughter. I never met th' man. Don't know where he lives, even. You know 'im?"

"Yes, I've met Justin, but I have no idea where he lives." She blew her nose to hide her tears, remembering Rosalie's beautiful coffin and the yellow and white daisies. She knew that one had been made by Justin but hadn't yet connected it with Tikki. And now he had done the same for Orley. Would her heart tear apart right there in front of Ray?

"They were gonna do an autopsy today. Standard procedure in a case like this, but there's no reason for thinkin' it more'n a heart attack."

Ray stood up and stretched. "Well, Jennifer, if you'd be willing to testify, we could nail Coop and Connie with this thing an' put an end to all th' nonsense that's cookin' up."

"Oh, Ray! I can't! I promised I wouldn't! I shouldn't have even told you, but—"

"I'm glad you did. Anything those two say I weigh pretty careful just on principle. But they were in a pretty sorry state, and it was a sure thing they didn't do it to each other. The fire seemed more down their alley than Tikki's, but there was nothin' more'n their version t' go on. It helps to know the real story. It sure would trim their tailfeathers some t' pin an arson and manslaughter charge on 'em, though! Sure y' won't change your mind?"

She paused a moment but then shook her head. "No. Nothing I could say would bring Orley back. And my promise was important to Tikki. But will you try to stop the men from going after him?"

"I'll do my best. I think once they dry up, they'll see things different. I'll keep my eye on 'em, though—don't worry. And remember, Tikki's not called 'The Fox' for nothin'!"

Orley's burial was a simple graveside service. Jennifer was surprised by the number of Clevis people who came, many of them church folk who had stood by at Rosalie's funeral just a few weeks earlier.

The coffin showed the same rustic but careful craftsmanship as Rosalie's, but with more heft and solidness, as though to give him in death what he lacked in life. Jennifer looked at it often during the brief service, as if to decipher a message out of this most recent token from Tikki's hand.

The long fingers of fear kept after Jennifer day and night, giving her little rest. A letter she received about this time didn't add to her peace of mind. From the Ace Detective Agency, it was a rumpled, smudged missive asking for information about Tikki Granger on behalf of their client, someone with a foreign-sounding name. She read it through twice, a feeling of nausea gripping her as she visualized a fat, greasy, cigar-chomping private eye in the hire of thugs in black limousines. Was the letter a trick, a ploy to get her to reveal his whereabouts? Well, she didn't know where he was and didn't intend to aid and abet the enemy in any way. So after dashing off a quick reply saying she couldn't help them and would give no information without knowing the ends to which it would be used, she ripped up the letter and threw it in the wastebasket. The matter troubled her for a while, but as the days went by, she decided that Ace had given up on her as a source of information.

To her relief, things settled down in town. Ray had evidently hinted to Coop and Connie that he had their number, for they had remarkably little more to say concerning their supposed ill treatment. But though the would-be vigilantes were not as vocal, their mood was still ugly. An area-wide surveillance network was talked about, and Jennifer lived in constant dread that Tikki hadn't gone far enough away. In mining country, things have a way of happening by design or "accident," whichever best suits the occasion. She recalled the hulks who had come into the schoolroom after Tikki. Nola Mae had reassured her after that incident: "Don't worry about Tikki. He can take care of himself." These words came back now to give her hope and comfort.

26   Jennifer had thought that telling Corey she wouldn't marry him would be difficult, but it turned out to be relatively easy. Not that he took it calmly or didn't make a fuss, and not that she liked hurting him. But making the decision was easy, and so she felt right and good about telling him.

She had had to sort through her feelings and motives and desires, a difficult procedure, but one through which she felt unerringly guided. She came out certain of several things: her reasons for marrying Corey had been based largely on convenience, lack of alternatives, and a desire for prestige; she neither loved nor felt truly comfortable with him; and even though he fit many of the items on her "marriage agenda," uniting with him for the sake of ministry would be a mockery of what they would be trying to accomplish in the name of God.

Yes, deciding about Corey was easy. It was in thinking about Tikki that she felt out of control. But even here, things were taking on definition. She knew that she loved him as she could never love Corey, but she also realized that marriage would probably be out of the question. No matter how she felt about him, she could not—would not—marry him if he were not a Christian. Then, too, she knew Tikki well enough to take seriously his statement that he might never come back. She was also aware that there was very little she actually knew about him. Even the recent revelations only deepened the mystery surrounding him. But she did feel sure she could finally sort out the genuine from the phony. His isolation and all his mean, offensive behavior, though serious, were simply improvised bandages to cover gaping wounds. He had crawled away from some unbearable pain and hidden inside a barnacle-encrusted shell where he could shield himself from the encroachments of the world around him. With Rosalie and Orley, and with her when she was ill, he had crept out and become vulnerable, but by *his* choice.

But recognizing this only produced more conflict for Jennifer. Corey would (and did) say that Tikki was a sinner in need of salvation—period. Don't get emotionally involved. She herself longed to find Tikki and just say "It's all right! It's all right!", but that seemed wrong, too. What was right? she asked. What, before God, was right? Then, too, sometimes she didn't even care to know what was right. She felt a bit annoyed with God and His inscrutable ways. Was Tikki just a temptation dangled before her to divert her from her path of righteousness? Or was he a test, as Isaac was to Abraham? Kill the thing within you that you love best in order to prove your devotion to God? If you don't, God may do the killing for you.

But it was before she had resolved her unrest about Tikki

that she decided about Corey and told him she wouldn't marry him. Only slightly nervous before she broke the news to him, she felt such a peace immediately afterward that the storm of reaction from Corey hardly touched her at all. In thinking about it later, she marvelled at that. Perhaps her exposure to Tikki's assorted rages had inured her somewhat. Corey couldn't hold a candle to one of Tikki's minor gusts. But Jennifer decided she had been unaffected because what she was doing was right. Nothing Corey said could change that.

He said plenty, though. He put forth a whole catalog of grievances to which she listened patiently and agreed or disagreed where appropriate: he had invested too much time in her for her to run out on him now; she had been unfaithful to him and to God; she had been corrupted and drawn from him by Nola Mae's ungodly ways; she was immature, unstable, spiritually and in every other way unfit to be a minister's wife, and the sooner she amended her course and reconsidered her decision, the better off they would both be.

While all of this was boiling around her, Jennifer caught a glimpse of a little patch of blue sky with a swallow tacking back and forth; her heart went out and flew with the bird for just a few minutes, but it was enough, and she could continue her patient listening.

Nola Mae was spending quite a bit of time by her record player, listening to her song and staring at nothing in particular.

> Waters ripple and flow,
>   Slowly passes each day;
> Faithless lover of mine,
>   Stay no longer away.

Dear one, well dost thou know
  Why fond lovers must part:
Wherefore falters thy faith?
  Why so timid thy heart?

Dearest lover come back;
  End the vigil I keep.
Thine, the key to my heart,
  Mine, without thee to weep!

When the mountain shall turn,
  When the vict'ry is thine,
Then my happiness dawns,
  Then shall freedom be mine.

Lo, the mountain has turn'd,
  Now the vict'ry is thine;
Now my happiness dawns,
  Now shall freedom be mine!

Jennifer heard these words from one perspective, Nola
Mae from quite a different one. Jeremy Tybolt had told
her that indeed she had been replaced by Miss New, and
her emotions had already swung from anger to deep disappointment over the loss of what was for her a genuine
attachment. She tried not to show her distress, especially
in front of Jennifer, who was so caught up in her own
misery that she had little comfort to give. But a minor
incident brought about a significant change.

One warm, sunny morning, Nola Mae was outdoors
wandering aimlessly around the yard. After a bit, she called
toward the house.

"Jennifer! Come out here a minute."

"What do you want?"

"Come out and look at this."

"Look at what?" Whatever Nola Mae was peering at was
hidden behind some ferns, so Jennifer moved on down
the steps.

"It's a rabbit, and it isn't moving."

"What's the matter with it?" Jennifer asked.

"I don't know. It just lies there with its head on its paws." Nola Mae reached out to touch the animal. As she did so, it gave a lurch of fright as though to bound away but could do no more than flop over on its side. Nola Mae stroked its head with her fingers. "It's so soft!" she murmured.

"I don't see any marks where a dog or cat might have gotten it," Jennifer said. "It must be sick."

"Poor thing."

"Probably the best thing would be to let the cat out to put it out of its misery." Jennifer had things other than sick rabbits to occupy her and didn't want to become involved in a rescue attempt. "That's what I'd do," and she walked back into the house.

But in a few minutes, Nola Mae came in carrying the rabbit, and with a small sigh Jennifer rummaged about for a box and an old sheet. Mostly, though, she watched Nola Mae with growing interest. Nola Mae, who so seldom showed an ounce of pity for anything or anyone outside herself, was now bent over the little creature in the cardboard box. Jennifer turned away; but her heart had been touched, and she no longer saw herself as the only sufferer in the household.

Within two hours the rabbit was dead, and without a word Nola Mae carefully wrapped it in a plastic bag and took it outside to bury it.

When she came in, Jennifer was ready, and with only a slight hesitation, Nola Mae found tearful release in her arms.

They talked much that day, each coming to a new understanding and appreciation of the other. Jennifer judiciously refrained from giving out any "spiritual spaghetti," and just listened. Nola Mae listened, too, and Jennifer was surprised she was so supportive of her decision not to marry Corey—surprised that Nola Mae understood her feelings about him and about what she would be giving up. She was understanding, too, about the way things stood with Tikki, and even though Jennifer had been careful to keep her word to him, Nola Mae had guessed right away that she had been with him and that a major crisis was at hand.

That night, for the first time since they had begun living together, the women intentionally shared a meal. And it was very good.

| 27 | With each passing day Jennifer tried to buoy up her hopes that Tikki had retreated to a place of safety, or that the worst anyone would do was beat him up as he had beaten Coop and Connie, but still a sense of impending calamity hung over her. It was difficult to keep her mind on her teaching. She prayed for Tikki continuously and spent long hours with her Bible, often crossing the river after school and climbing to the place he had shown her that overlooked the gorge.

Corey was losing no opportunity to impress on her the judgment that God was laying up for her, often referring to Isaiah. She realized with a smile that they had been jousting these past two weeks along a battle line not overtly acknowledged by either of them. She had not told him she had been with Tikki that day in the woods, and he had not accused her of it. But both knew, and the battle was waged on this unspoken assumption.

But Jennifer decided to more closely inspect the wrath from God's hand of which Corey had warned, and so read through the entire Book of Isaiah. Her attention was captured by the many references to the mountain of the Lord as a place of righteousness and blessing for God's people. She stopped for a moment and looked out over the gorge to the magnificent panorama that seemed to stretch forever. Righteousness and blessing . . . maybe happiness and freedom, too, as in "Waters Ripple and Flow"?

There was judgment in Isaiah, yes, but stored up for those who turned away from the Lord to do evil. Had she turned away? She didn't think so. She was trying to be honest with herself and with God, and she was certainly crying out for His help.

As she read on, she became more and more caught up by the distressed prayers of the prophet on behalf of those who were hopelessly entangled in the repercussions of sin, and by the great love and compassion of God for His wayward children. Her whole heart entered into the passages, and the words became her own.

> Oh, that you would rend the heavens and come down,
> that the mountains would tremble before you! . . .

> "I revealed myself to those who did not ask for me;
> I was found by those who did not seek me.
> To a nation that did not call on my name,
> I said, 'Here am I, here am I.'
> All day long I have held out my hands
> to an obstinate people."

There it was—the Hound of Heaven, the God who patiently stands close by, holding out grace and love and mercy to the weak and blind of a world mired in bogs of its own making. He alone could help Tikki, but in her distress, she was acting as though worry would somehow save him. Even worse, she had not really wanted God to interfere in their relationship and was afraid of what He might do. If she were to offer him up as her Isaac, there would perhaps be no ram in the thicket, no staying of the knife thrust.

She bent her head and wept. *Oh, Tikki! I can't give you up! I've just found you. But if I don't, neither of us will possess the mountain. Everything is so complicated.*

She turned back to Genesis for the account of Abraham's testing, and again her attention was riveted. "So Abraham called that place 'The Lord will provide.' And to this day it is said, 'On the mountain of the Lord it will be provided.'"

At that point, her mountain began to turn.

The sun was low, but her heart was light as she finished singing with Isaiah:

> "Behold, I will create
>   new heavens and a new earth.
> The former things will not be remembered,
>   nor will they come to mind. . . .
> Before they call I will answer;
>   while they are still speaking I will hear.
> The wolf and the lamb will feed together,
>   and the lion will eat straw like the ox. . . .
> They will neither harm nor destroy
>   in all my holy mountain," says the Lord.

And when she crossed back over the river, the door of her cage now dangled from one hinge.

She heard the phone ringing as she stepped up on the porch. Nola Mae had evidently gone out, so she hurried in to get the call. It was Hubert Smith. "I got good news fer you, ma'am. You won't need t' worry about Tikki Granger ever agin!"

28 Winter in spring. Unsettled weather. A front passes through at nightfall. Then as the clouds roll off toward the east, the stars beckon to the heat of the earth and call it forth, while long silent tentacles of icy air slither across the landscape, settling in low areas such as river valleys to ravage the *magnum opus* of spring. Little brown centers on strawberry blossoms condemn them to barrenness; tomato plants melt down to a shapeless tangle; beans, cucumbers, squashes, and melons turn black under the frigid hand of frost. Winter is beautiful in its place, but out of bounds it becomes ugly, predacious.

Winter in spring. Clevis gardeners were not the only ones to suffer loss. Jennifer's heart was frozen, her landscape bleak and barren.

She had laid Tikki on the altar, God had accepted her offering, and she felt the rightness of it. She was not surprised; her grief did not spill over into outward display; she was not even angry with God. She did not think He had acted as her judge, handing down her just desserts. Nor had He put her through a Job-like wringer to test her devotion. Instead, she sensed a fundamental necessity to it all. As Tikki had said, "This is the way it has to be." And in this He was standing by her—with tears of His own. She could do nothing but clutch His hand, clinging with icy fingers to His cauterizing love.

After Hubert Smith finished his report, Jennifer phoned Ray to verify it. But Ray hadn't heard anything yet. Late the following day, however, he came by the house, and she knew at a glance it was true.

Ferreting out the information had been difficult, he said. The Jensen police referred him to the state police who sent him for some reason to the Estrùnd police who knew nothing of the affair. Then Randy Lindel said he'd heard from his cousin, who had a brother-in-law in Belleridge where the body had been found. Thus after an entire day of telephoning, Ray had finally collected what facts were known.

The body had been fished out of the Elk River. Ray carefully avoided describing its condition, but Jennifer's imagination filled in the details, once she heard the word "decomposed." The autopsy had shown water in his lungs, indicating he'd been alive when he hit the river. He might have been knocked unconscious and thrown in, or he could have slipped and fallen against rocks or even jumped from a bridge upstream. There was no way of telling. Several people had made "pretty sure" identification, but a man came forward who had known him quite well—well enough to recognize specific scars. Jennifer shivered and saw again the crooked white line along Tikki's thumb.

"I'm sorry," said Ray. "I wish it had been different. He wasn't all bad. But you know that." He pushed his hair back and chuckled. "Probably one of his biggest services was t' keep Hubert in line."

"Hubert? In line?"

"Yes. Hubert likes to take a nip once in a while, and Tikki found his little stash at the store and threatened to squeal to the powers-that-be at church if he got too high-handed in his dealings, especially with folks like Orley who were long on need and short on cash." He gave her a crooked grin as he opened the screen door. "Sorta like that Justin in some ways."

In a sense, nearly every death is a small, lonely affair. The rest of the world goes on as usual with its buying and selling, eating and lovemaking, untouched by the intense grief of the little band of mourners. They, too, will have their moments of sorrow, though not now.

But Jennifer's was a particularly lonely grief. Though Ellen and Nola Mae stood by her with comfort and love, no one mourned for Tikki. Orley and Rosalie would have wept with her, but they were now safely beyond tears. Kenny and Joey might have cared enough to salt away a couple of extra beers in his memory; other drinks, too, were lifted to his memory, but these in celebration.

However, the sun continued to rise each morning and set every night. And Corey made one more attempt to persuade her to marry him now that, as he supposed, the biggest obstacle was out of the way. He came to the door on a warm, pleasant evening and asked, "Would you like to go for a walk?"

He looked forlorn, and even though Jennifer suspected what he had in mind, she hadn't the heart to refuse. They walked toward the church, not along the schoolyard paths as Jennifer would have done, but on the sidewalks in deference to Corey's leather-tassled loafers. They talked about the balmy air, how green everything looked, plans for the church picnic, and how much Hubie Smith's new dog resembled its young owner.

When they reached the church, he took her into the cemetery to a stone bench from which they could see back through the scattered trees toward Duncan Creek. The disappearing sun set the sky awash with color. Plume-like clouds bore vivid hues of pink and rose and lilac against a backdrop ranging from yellow and green on one side through purest blue overhead to a deep rich velvet on the other. A painful kind of beauty, it made Jennifer ache for something that was at once joyous and terrible and magnificent, yet just out of reach. Not so much out of reach, perhaps, as fleeting. It came in the fullness of its majesty, but only for an instant, enough to say, "Yes, it's real," but too brief to say just what it was. And then it was gone, along with all the other transitory beauties of life, the *people* of life.

"Jennifer, I know how the events of the past few weeks have affected you. Actually, it's been months, when you look back. Even though you seemed to recover quickly from your illness, who knows what long-term effects were left? Then Rosalie's death hit you hard and undermined your, ah—your emotional well-being. It's no wonder you've come apart at the seams lately."

Jennifer thought about that, picturing herself as an old doll, plaster head and floppy cloth body with sawdust trickling out of weak places along the seams. Her face would be checked with age, but her eyes would still open and shut as she stood or lay down. Or remain permanently open if she sat forgotten in a dark corner, shielded from the dust of decades by a thin piece of tissue paper.

"I know I've said some harsh things, and I—I'm—sorry if I hurt you. You haven't been yourself, and I guess I overreacted. I want you to know that I do understand what you've gone through and how you feel, and that it will take time for you to get over . . . what you've been through, and get back to normal."

Corey? Understand? She smiled to herself but said nothing.

"I've prayed for you a great deal this past week, and I feel certain that the Lord will help you thread your way through all this emotional stress to the place where you'll see plainly once again His will for your life."

He stopped and took her hand. "I do love you very much, Jennifer, and the Lord has made clear to me that you are the one He has chosen to be my wife. The things that have happened, the words that were said, those are all behind us now, and we can go on to become one flesh, united in the work the Lord has called us to. God has promised to give us beauty for ashes, joy for mourning, praise instead of heaviness. His yoke is easy, His burden light."

His voice was low, trembling with emotion, and his hands holding hers were damp with perspiration. "Come to me, dearest. Come and complete my joy. 'Forgetting those things that are behind, press on toward the mark for the prize of the high calling of God in Christ Jesus.'

Forget—*forget*—put out of your mind the things that have come between us, and let God join together what man cannot put asunder."

Jennifer felt pity for Corey. He needed a wife; the demands of the flesh were heavy upon him, and now she grasped the spiritual import for him of her answer. His desperation was plain: never before had he suggested, even intimated, that he might have been wrong in any way. Nor was she surprised by the heavy artillery of God's will that he had leveled at her, but it was a bit much, even for Corey.

Could she marry him? The thought surprised her as though it were brand-new. To say yes would be so easy— almost as easy as saying no. Perhaps it was God's will, and He had anesthetized her so she wouldn't think too much and just accept it. She knew Corey would love her and care for her in his own way, and along would come the tall blond sons and willowy daughters she had always envisioned. So easy . . .

The color had faded from the darkening sky. A wood thrush set up its evening carol in the gathering gloom, and the sound pierced Jennifer's ice-clad heart with an ache that brought tears to her eyes. *Can you live with that—for my sake?* The last words Tikki had said to her. *For my sake.* She drew a quivery breath. Yes, for his sake she had to be true to herself, to the person she was before God. *For freedom Christ has set us free. Stand fast, therefore. . . .*

The darkness obscured the color rising in Corey's neck and face as she explained to him once again that she could not marry him. He controlled himself, however, and tried to reason patiently with her, but when he found he could not make a dent in her resolve, his composure disintegrated.

"You are in willful rebellion against the Lord, making a mockery of your commitment to Him! You are setting up

Tikki Granger as some sort of god, an idol, and burning the Devil's incense to his memory! But God will not be mocked, and you are deceiving yourself if you think you can hide from His wrath behind your flimsy rationale of our not being suited to each other. Just when you should be stripping off the filthy garments of unrighteousness, you're piling sin upon sin and heaping judgment on your head!"

As he ranted on, Jennifer felt the incongruity of it all here in the cemetery amid the beauty of the descending night. Although aware that she herself was a direct, though partial, cause of his distress—not just now in her refusal, but because of all she had fostered in their relationship since last fall—still she was angry. Angry at the harshness of his displeasure and at the falsity underlying this attempt at reconciliation.

But with as much charity as she could muster, she sought to extricate herself quickly and gracefully. "I'm sorry, Corey. I've brought you a lot of pain and disappointment, and if there's blame to be laid, I'm willing to take it all, in the eyes of men at least. Before God I am at peace, absolutely sure I've made the right decision. I only hope that someday soon, when you find the right girl to be your wife, you'll see it, too . . . no, please don't rail any further. You've said everything you could to warn me, and anything more will only put you, as well as me, on dangerous ground before God."

And so, the painful conversation at an end, they walked in silence back to the house, each feeling grieved and hurt, but for reasons as hidden from each other as ships passing in the night.

As a gemstone found among paper clips and thumbtacks, so was a quote Jennifer happened on in a school trade catalog before it was consigned to the wastebasket. The name "Solzhenitsyn" caught her eye, and she read eagerly as the short excerpt, employed to hawk art supplies, spoke to her condition.

> Art can warm even a chilled and sunless soul to an exalted spiritual experience. Through art we occasionally receive—indistinctly, brieflly—revelations the likes of which cannot be achieved by rational thought.
>
> It is like that small mirror of legend: you look into it but instead of yourself you glimpse for a moment the Inaccessible, a realm forever beyond reach. And your soul begins to ache.

So in addition to her Bible, Jennifer gazed long into the looking glass of Art, feeding the beauty-starved tissues of her soul and seeing as never before the One who is Beauty. And the more she took in, the hungrier she became. She found the boundary lines of Truth to be far wider than she had supposed and the enclosed meadows full of delights that were hers for the taking.

She talked much with Nola Mae on the subject, and from there to matters spiritual and philosophic, both of them listening and learning from each other. Even though initiating such conversations still made her uncomfortable, Jennifer was more honest and relaxed and no longer felt obliged to inject "religious words" into every discussion or to press for change in Nola Mae. In turn, Nola Mae felt free to share her own beliefs, especially her credo, taken from Keats: "'Beauty is truth, truth beauty'; that is all ye know on earth, and all ye need to know." In the early months of their acquaintance, Jennifer would have summarily dismissed this as outright heresy, but now . . . She had glimpsed the wonders and marvels of a far-off land and could not write them off as invalid hallucinations. But neither was she willing to stop at an equation of Beauty with Truth, and so they talked. In this climate Nola Mae blossomed as both teacher and listener and was more inclined than before to consider the impact of Jennifer's life on her own. She still could not see that Jennifer's proscribed lifestyle had brought any less grief than her own had to herself, but she was deeply impressed by the unfolding of an exquisite flower from the ice-encased bud she had thought would surely atrophy and drop away.

With the return of the sun to her life, Jennifer began to assess the impact on her life of those she had loved and lost through the year. For one thing, she now knew loneliness as an absence of something positive rather than an indefinable lack. In that one brief day of genuine companionship with Tikki, her concept of friendship was forever expanded to take in far vistas of the soul hitherto unseen. Just thinking about the warmth of his arm around her brought an ache for the aliveness she had felt, the brightness of a world shared with one's beloved. Yes, she now knew loneliness for what it truly was, but better to be lonely than never to have had a friend. And both Rosalie and Tikki had taught her to see and hear in ways she never had before. The art of hearing learned from a deaf child. The art of gentleness learned from the most explosive person she had ever known. And Orley, in buckling beneath the stress of life, had taught her endurance. All three had been truly beautiful people, and she would carry their marks proudly on her soul throughout all eternity.

Beauty and Truth. They had come to her in many guises throughout the year, and the pain of all her losses became for her a monument to the special revelation her friends had brought to her life. "'Beauty is truth, truth beauty.'" She could add to that, "*Pain* is beauty is truth," because all of these attributes were swallowed up in the One who is the Lamb that was slain, the bright Morning Star, the Alpha and the Omega.

29 The gray catbird whisked first this way, then that, always with one of its black eyes on Raskolnikov, who was making his appointed rounds among the shrubs and brush that enclosed the yard. The two measured each other, the one meowing an imprecatory warning, the other responding with silent, whiskered disdain. When the cat had padded off to a safe distance, the bird set up his variegated song that announced to other potential intruders just who he was and where he stood.

Raskolnikov had gotten out when Jennifer left the house to run down to the store. Tomorrow was Nola Mae's birthday, and she didn't want to use the one long-forgotten package of hamburg in the freezer. She was excited that Nola Mae had agreed to choose what she would like Jennifer to cook for her birthday dinner. That she felt free to select an entree as complex as lasagna, knowing full well how long it took to make, said something about the friendship and trust that was building between them.

Jennifer needed to make the dish today, not only to allow the flavors to mingle overnight, but also because tomorrow was Sunday, a day too hectic for cooking. And with Nola Mae gone today, Jennifer could make cheesecake as an extra surprise.

She wanted it to be a special meal. The school year would end in just two-and-a-half days, and with it would come a parting of their ways. Nola Mae had applied for and gotten a teaching position in Charleston, a little closer to the center of her universe. Jennifer had several applications out but had heard nothing definite yet. She, too, wanted to leave Clevis as soon as possible. Leaving would be hard in many ways. She would miss her friends, especially Ellen and all the children she had come to love at school and church. Also, moving away from the river would be tantamount to a spiritual dislocation, and now that she was no longer afraid to roam the woods, she had become

174

attached to several lovely little places, whether by a stream, or near an old moss-and-fern-cloaked log, or simply under a particularly hospitable oak. Having acquired her own bird and flower books, she was doing quite well with the more common species, and from time to time she even tried her hand at sketching.

Jennifer knew she would also miss Nola Mae's records and books. She had already made up her mind, however, that a sound system and collection of her own would be a good spiritual investment, and she was going to ask Nola Mae for a list of records to add to those she had decided she must have: Brahms' *Requiem*, *Appalachian Spring*, the Britten *Te Deum*, and any old collection that included "Waters Ripple and Flow."

And, of course, leaving Nola Mae would be hard. Neither of them spoke of it, but both felt the pain of the imminent rupture. The birthday fete would be a sort of unspoken farewell dinner as well, and even though Nola Mae was going out on a date in the evening, it would be the appropriate occasion to ceremonialize their friendship.

The catbird flounced about with his eye on another intruder, giving forth short segments of song to warn him to stay on the porch instead of coming near the shrubbery.

On her way back from the store, Jennifer saw him, too, and cast about in her mind who the well-dressed stranger might be. A school-supply salesman? Not likely on a Saturday. A Mormon or Jehovah's Witness? They normally operated in pairs, didn't they? The minister friend Corey had said was coming to visit? Someone looking for Nola Mae? Well, she hoped he wouldn't stay long. She had her cheese grated and garlic and onions and peppers all cut up and ready to go.

"Hello—can I help you? I'm Jennifer Darrow."

The stranger stood and smiled as she came toward the steps. He was tall with close-cropped dark hair, and his shirt and tie and starkly conservative sports jacket sat elegantly on his broad shoulders. "Hi. Nathan Sevasty. Do you remember me? I was in the area and thought I'd look you up."

Jennifer's brain worked frantically. Nathan Sevasty. Who in the world was he? Someone she knew from college, or high school even? He looked familiar, the name sounded familiar, but . . . Sevasty. She was sure she had heard that name before, but where? That letter, the one from Ace Detective Agency? There had been an odd name in that. Could this be a detective? No, it couldn't be—the image was all wrong.

He seemed to be watching her closely as he remarked on how pretty the town was this time of year. His voice . . . his eyes . . . Little electric shocks began to stab her legs, her stomach, her jaw. She grew weak and the man's face began to swim. His eyes reflected concern, and he reached out to support her.

"Tikki?" she whispered.

He shook his head. "No. Tikki is dead," he said softly. "I'm Nathan Sevasty."

She searched his face with wide and panicky eyes. "You *are* Tikki!" She barely sounded the words.

Again he spoke, firmly this time. "Tikki is dead."

Suddenly she broke away from his supporting hold and grabbed for his right hand, the grocery bag dropping unheeded from her arms. When she saw the jagged scar, her body shook with sobs. He put his arms around her and held her, gently stroking her hair. After a few moments he took a handkerchief from his pocket and lifted her face to wipe her tears.

He leaned over and picked up the bag and peered inside. "Some o' Hubert's finest horsemeat?"

She laughed. "I'm making lasagna for Nola Mae's birthday tomorrow—just let me stick it in the frig."

"And she's not afraid you'll poison her?" He followed her in. "You an' she must be gettin' on some better. I understand old Teabag dumped her."

"How is it you know everything?" She closed the refrigerator and nestled in his arms once again. "Oh, Tikki! I love you so much!"

He pushed her back gently and held her face between his hands. "Nathan," he corrected. "Nathan. Say it. Nathan Sevasty."

"Nathan. Nathan Sevasty. Nathan Sevasty," she repeated solemnly, the significance of it finally sinking in. "That is your real name, isn't it?" Her voice was again just a whisper.

He nodded, and the trace of a shadow flickered over his face. Then he took her hand and drew her toward the door. "Let's go up to the pines and talk."

She pulled him back. "It's almost lunchtime. Are you hungry? Do you want me to make you a sandwich?"

He shook his head with a grin. "No. I just had Matt Cooper serve me up his Saturday special . . . which he did with all deference and servility."

"Oh, Tik . . . Nathan, you're absolutely wicked! No, you're not. That's too close to what Corey would say. Let's go."

"Fix yourself something if you're hungry. I can wait."

"I couldn't eat now if my life depended on it!"

They reached the top of the knoll, and Jennifer looked at him ruefully. "I should've brought a blanket along. You'll ruin your beautiful clothes!"

"They're just for effect anyway. Don't expect me to appear on your doorstep like this every day! . . . Do you know what was hardest for me to do, even harder than kissing you good-by? Burning my chamois shirt. It felt like I was throwing my right arm into the fire."

"I'm surprised it didn't disintegrate before it even hit the flames!"

"Oh, come now! I got it cleaned just for your benefit. Didn't you notice?"

"Yes, I did. I'm teasing you. I'm just so wildly happy, nothing else matters! You're alive and here with me!"

She looked at him with shining eyes. "Nathan Sevasty. That's a nice name." But a small frown marked her brow as she thought of her cigar-chomping correspondent. Had the name of the "other party" been Sevasty? She had been so anxious to rid herself of the menacing letter that she had hardly looked at the name. "You didn't send me a letter from the Ace Detective Agency, did you? Just as a joke?"

His puzzled look was answer enough.

"No—never mind. Will you tell me now who Nathan Sevasty is?" The shadow flickered again. "You don't have to," she hastily added.

He was silent a moment, studying his pressed-together fingertips. "I'm not sure where to begin."

"Wherever it's easiest. You could tell me a little today and more, maybe, another time. Can you say where you've been and how Tikki came to be reported dead?"

He laughed shortly. "That's easy enough. I identified the body."

"You!"

"Yes. A dark-bearded man about my size and shape turned up dead in the Elk River. Someone started suggesting it was Tikki Granger. All I had to do was walk in, look over the body, comment, with just the properly grave expression, on scars and birthmarks, sign my name, and Tikki was officially dead. I even attended the burial!"

"You didn't!"

"It was a bit strange, but actually, Tikki fell mortally ill

178

that day right here in the pine grove after Rosalie's funeral, and he died on the way up Plaggett Mountain."

"Died—and was resurrected."

He looked up at her. "Yes." He said it very quietly, almost to himself.

They both sat silent. "Well—" rousing himself, "let's get on with this thing. It's like having a tooth pulled without novocaine." He smiled wryly and lay back with hands behind his head.

"Nathan Alexander Sevasty. Born thirty-two years ago of Jonathan and Caroline Sevasty in one of the more affluent suburbs of Pittsburgh. Caroline—violinist and music teacher before marriage, retired to become wife and helpmeet to the president of a company that manufactures musical instruments. Parents both straight, hard-working; older brother Justin straight, hard—"

"Justin?"

He nodded. "Yes. Justin was a good kid. He'd just started med school last I knew, over twelve years ago. When Orley and Rosalie began wringing a little something worthwhile out of me, I decided it ought to be Justin who got the credit and not me.

"Justin—straight, hard-working; Nathan inclined more toward fun and games. I went to school but didn't know what for, except that the night life there was more promising than at home with the rest of the family.

"I should tell you about my grandfather, by the way. He's one bright spot in this tale. He was a feisty old gentleman who grew up under the czar in Russia and managed to escape by a whisker during the revolution. His name was Alexander Sevastyanov, but he shortened it to Sevasty when he got over here."

"So you *were* saying things in Russian to Galina!"

He grinned and scratched his head. "I'll have to figure some way to make up to her for that. My dad used to get

179

really angry when Grandfather taught us boys Russian obscenities. 'What would Mother say if she were alive?' he'd sputter. And Grandfather would explode with his great roaring laughter. 'Plenty!' he'd say and wait till Dad was almost out of sight before starting in again. It was just a big joke, and he loved to laugh.

"He taught me to love the outdoors. He'd take us camping and fishing and show us which plants had healing properties. Justin wanted to be a doctor from the time he was six months old, so he lapped it all up. But I just stored it away as interesting but not very practical."

"But it ended up saving my life," Jennifer said.

"Not really. It only made you a little more comfortable." His face took on grimness. "Here I was, giving you a strong narcotic, and Frank Stanley was afraid to give you even a weak antibiotic! If he'd been handy, I'd 've throttled him on the spot. As it is, I don't know what kept me from burning down his store!"

"Poor Frank! He means well, but he's just timid."

"If you had died—"

"But I didn't, and God kept you from doing damage."

Again he said simply, "Yes. . . . Anyway, Grandfather and I got on well together. He understood me and I listened to him more than to my folks. I even look like him. I didn't realize it till I first saw myself in a mirror after my hair and beard grew out. Grandmother probably would have fainted if she'd seen me then."

"Did you learn the birds and trees and flowers from him, too?"

"A good many, but he gave me more than just names. I got a deep love for the natural order of things. He wasn't what you'd call a God-fearing man," he grinned, "but he had a strong sense of the spiritual dimension of life. He was a remarkable old man. And if he'd lived a little longer, things might've been different."

He stopped and drew several deep breaths. Jennifer got up on her knees and moved over in front of him. "Don't. Don't say any more if it hurts too much."

He looked at her with tortured eyes and held her hands tightly, his voice husky. "I've got to. I need to. It's like a poison that's been eating away at me all these years, and the only way to get rid of it is to say the words. And you're the only person I can say them to."

In answer, she held his head tight to her breast.

Down the hill a voice called out, "Jennifer! Are you home?" It was Hilda Smith.

 **30** "Oh, no! I'd better go down, If I don't, she's just apt to come up here. I know she will!"

"Wait. You stay. I'll go down. Just keep out of sight." And he went noiselessly down off the side of the knoll toward the gorge. A few minutes later she heard two voices by the house but couldn't make out what either was saying. In five minutes he was back up, a smile on his face.

"She's gone."

"What did you say?"

"I told her I was an insurance adjuster looking for Jennifer Darrow. I wanted to speak with her concerning a $100,000 life insurance policy she had taken out on a Tikki Granger. I asked if she knew where I might find Miss Darrow. She looked as though she'd just shaken hands with an electric eel! First time I ever saw her at a loss for words. She promised to send you home if she found you, and I said I'd be waiting near the river bank. It'll take her a spell just to figure out which side of her mouth to talk out of and quite a bit more to spread the news. We'll have an hour or two before she's back, and that should be enough." The dogged look returned to his face, but Jennifer sat down beside him, chuckling over his delay tactic.

"Now cut that out!" he said. "You're supposed to be serious!" But his eyes were party to her laughter. "Where were we?"

"I'm sorry. It just tickles me to see Hilda's mouth plugged, even if only for a moment. I'll be good! You were saying you got along with your grandfather better than with—"

"—with my folks. Right. They just didn't know how to handle me. It wasn't that they didn't love me or care what I did. It just seemed they did everything wrong. They were picky about trifles but pushed me into things I wasn't ready for. And they let me have all the money I wanted. In addition, I had access to a stack of bonds when I turned eighteen. That approach worked fine for Justin. He was cut from their kind of cloth. But it was all wrong for me. You couldn't have designed a more perfect setup for a wild-eyed college kid, and I cavorted about measuring the size of the pasture and the height of the fences."

"Was your grandpa still alive then? Did he know what was happening?"

"*Grandfather.* Never 'Gramps' or 'Grandpa.' He demanded respect. . . . No, he died my last year of high school, climbing a mountain at age eighty-three, just as he wanted to die—quick and doing something worthwhile."

He took a firmer grip on her hand. "There were girls, too. Lots of them, in and out of bed. . . . But then, one came along who was different. She had a brain, for one thing; she was beautiful and sensitive. She loved music, and I began to appreciate my parents for cramming all that music down my throat. I could almost sound intelligent on the subject. Within six months we were engaged. My parents were happy, too, even though I still had two years of school to go. They liked Lynn. She played trios and quartets with them and had them eating out of her hand. And seeing me more settled pleased them, too.

"But one thing bothered me—I had never been able to get her to go to bed with me. I was crazy about her and respected her, but there was enough of the Devil still in me to want to get her to see things my way."

He was getting progressively more tense and swallowing frequently, but Jennifer could think of no better way to help him than just to sit with her fingers entwined in his. It seemed strange, hearing of this girl he had loved and holding herself up in comparison. She felt plain and dull and untalented, no match for Nathan's long-ago lover.

"There was a big affair one night at a country club, a wedding reception or fund-raising dinner—I don't remember what. But I'd been with Lynn all day at a lake and was feeling pretty high, and after a few drinks I decided to go for it. A friend was there who I knew used drugs, so I got what I wanted from him and then went to the bar to fix Lynn a drink."

He was trembling, his voice becoming more and more unsteady. Jennifer clung hard to his hands.

"She—she wasn't much of a drinker, so I couldn't make it strong or she wouldn't go past the first sip. But vodka covers up pretty well, and—it was in a Coke glass and looked like Coke, and—I slipped the tab of acid—into the glass—and—oh, God—she—she drank it down—" He looked steadily at the ground, beads of perspiration on his forehead.

"She—she looked at me sort of panicky and headed for the restroom. I thought—I began to realize what I had done, and I followed her. I waited outside the restroom—and counted the women who went in and came out—there were seven. I counted every one. The last one to come out said to her husband, 'There's a girl in there on the floor, dead drunk! In a nice place like this!' Seven women. *And not one of them would help her!*" He took several deep breaths.

"I ran in then, but she was already dead . . . and *I* killed her." His voice was barely a whisper. "The only girl I ever really loved, and I killed her." He suddenly swung around to face Jennifer and gripped her arms, searching her streaming face with wounded eyes. *"I killed her! What do you think about that?"*

Sobbing, Jennifer reached up and stroked his face and hair. "It's all right, darling, it's all right!" she whispered.

With a wrenching sob, he crushed her in his arms, and they sat rocking back and forth in a grief finally shared. A wood pewee flew to an overhead branch and gave forth his plaintive cry, and for a brief moment the whole world seemed to be weightless at the lifting of the burden. Coalesced through pain, the two clung to each other, and there hung over them a soft luminosity that brought healing and release to their individual souls.

Finally, Nathan continued. "I think I could have borne it if my parents had been supportive, but the only thing they had to say—after *two days*—was 'How could you *do* this to us? What will people say?' That was too much, and I took off.

"At first all I wanted to do was get away. It didn't much matter whether I lived or died. But I could hear Grandfather lecturing me on the cowardice of killing myself, so I had to figure out another alternative. I managed to get my securities and redeposited them down here under the name of Alexander Sevastyanov. Then I hid in the hills, away from family for one reason, the rest of the world for another. I learned pretty quick how to survive, and most people learned pretty quick that they'd better stay out of my way."

"Where did you come by the name Tikki Granger?" Jennifer asked.

"I saw it on an old grave marker, and it suited my mood that day, so I became Tikki.

184

"Things went along pretty much the same for several years. Mostly I tried not to stay in one place too long. The pain let up, but the anger and bitterness went on festering and kept Tikki alive and well.

"Probably the first person I went out of my way to help was Orley—I guess because he was so vulnerable and a magnet for trouble. Sara was near death at the time, and I did a lot of the farm work so he could be with her."

Jennifer looked up eagerly. "What kind of a woman was she? Rosalie showed me her picture, and I wished so much I could have met her."

"I went into the house only once while she was alive and was out again in less than five minutes. She took hold of my hand, and she knew—she *knew!* I couldn't stand it. Orley thought I was allergic to other folks' troubles, and I just let him go on thinking that. Rosalie was determined to be my friend, whether I liked it or not, lumping me together with Mouse and her infinite parade of kittens. She had a lot of her mother in her."

Jennifer sat up at the mention of kittens. " 'Eeny, Meeny, Miney, and there ain't no Mo!' *You* told her that!" She laughed aloud at the memory.

"She said that to you? Never forgot a thing!"

"She taught you sign language, didn't she?" Jennifer said.

A wry smile appeared. "The early stages of the taming of Tikki Granger. Dragged my heels all the way, I did, but she won in the end . . . how did you know, though? I made sure I never talked to her in the schoolyard."

"You used it several times, but I never realized it or put it all together till after our day together."

"I did? When?"

"The night of the fight in the classroom, to tell me to end the class right away, and again while we were looking at the deer, and then with Orley."

185

"Hmm. Rosalie snuck one over on us both."

"Was the 'Just-Friend' sign your idea?"

"No, that's pure Rosalie. I watched her play around with different combinations, but when she hit on that one, she had Orley and me jumping rope with it before she was through. That's why I was so busted up when Orley came out with it after we found him."

"I still miss her terribly," Jennifer said. "This last part of the school year has seemed so empty without her."

He put his arm around her and held her close, and each was quiet with a particular set of remembrances. He looked at her and smiled. "Then you moved in on me, and I didn't have a chance. If Rosalie was the number one punch, you were the number two."

A puzzled frown fastened on her face. "I don't understand that. All I can remember is being deathly afraid of you. What made you notice me at all?"

"What made me *notice* you! Just think about it: a teacher—one with religion, and destined for the position of Mrs. Worldchanger. To say nothing of your tie-in with Nola Mae! I noticed you, all right—the diversional possibilities were endless. You were one of the 'straights,' the 'very straights,' a representative of the Seven Women, and I was going to make you pay dearly. But you threw me a curve the night you took me in. I never expected that."

"You didn't expect me to take you in? Then why'd you come to my place? Why not to someone you knew might help you?"

He was silent a moment. "You don't know the twisted appetite bitterness has, the lengths it will go to feed itself." He paused again. "The river was up after the storm, but I needed to get across. I'd already hiked twenty miles or more in the storm on an empty stomach, and the temperature was dropping fast. I decided to go in above the ford, hoping to fetch out somewhere near it, but the river was too high and swift. I got bashed against a log snag some-where behind Smiths'. I still could have made it home, but I decided to knock on your door just for the satisfaction of having it slammed in my face, by you or Nola Mae, it didn't much matter. But you didn't slam it . . .

"I tried to get things back on a nasty keel with your night class, but then you went and got sick."

Jennifer recalled her terror the afternoon Tikki walked in on her. "In my wildest dreams I wouldn't have imagined you as a nurse," she smiled. "You certainly didn't have to take care of me."

He shook his head. "It wasn't you—it was Lynn. And the sicker you got, the more essential it was that you not die. It was your life for hers." Jennifer put her head down. "I'm sorry—I've hurt you." But she shook her head.

"It all makes sense now," she said. "I don't think you realized how much of Nathan you were letting me see that weekend. I didn't understand till later that that was the real you, but now it all seems so right and good." She added softly, "And you did save my life. You made your exchange."

"No . . . that guilt was not to be dealt with so easily. But it was enough that you were alive."

"Tell me—the people at the hospital were sure you must have had some sort of medical training to do such a good job on that tracheotomy. How did you know what to do?"

He smiled. "I did one on Orley's cow once, but she up and died after a bit anyway. It was your only hope, so I had to do it, that's all . . . and I hope to God I never have to face another one!" he added fervently. "After it was all over, it shook me when I realized how much I really did care that you were alive. I didn't want to love you. I didn't think it was possible for me to survive if I allowed myself to love."

Jennifer was quiet, sifting through the implications. "You

really might have taken me off somewhere that day I met you on the road outside of Plum, wouldn't you?"

The dark shadows again played over his face. "Yes. It hurts to say it, but yes, I might have." Abruptly he turned, anguish in his voice. "Jennifer, I swear to you before all that is holy and good, I will never ever touch your body with any trespass unless or until we're married! That is my vow before God!"

She was shaken by his vehemence, but looking into his eyes, she responded solemnly, "I promise not to make it difficult for you." She realized, however, that it would not be an easy promise to keep.

---

31 A green Volvo began the long climb out of Jensen. The edges of the steep, winding road still bore traces of the winter's overlay of sand and salt, but the hillsides were resplendent in new green finery, set off here and there by the darker tones of rhododendron foliage with its scattered brooches of pink blossoms.

The day was splendid—warm, a few fleecy clouds blown along by a temperate breeze, the quintessence of spring in Appalachia. Lambs gamboling alongside their stolid mothers in rail-enclosed pastures. An old woman out foraging in the woods for garlicky ramps. A teenaged girl riding bareback on her slick and shiny steed. The doors and windows of a trailer open wide in the hope that the drab interior would be renewed by the perfumed zephyr.

The small car carefully negotiated the switchbacks and climbed to the top of Foar's Knob. If its occupants had been of a mind to sightsee, they might have stopped at the turnout and looked back over the folded landscape toward the valley that held Jensen in sheltered safekeeping. A magnificent view, even in winter; the toiling crew that had broken out the pass after the big storm had been compensated in part by the spectacular panorama.

But the two in the car had no eyes for the view. Their minds were far away from panoramas, oblivious to the spring flowers of pasture and roadside. Their faces bore the set vagueness of far-off thoughts, whether of sorrow or anxiety or dread one could not tell.

One of them held a piece of paper, a rumpled letter with gray smudges that gave off a faint cigar odor, the hallmark of Ace Detective Agency. Although the contents of the letter had been memorized, the missive itself was gripped as though it were a talisman that would bring them safely to their destination.

And so the two crossed the divide and began the tortuous descent into Clevis.

When Randy Lindel came over from the hardware store to get the mail, he stopped at the window to talk to Frieda Copp, the postmistress. "Whose car is that out front—the Volvo?"

Frieda shook her head with the annoyance of a nosy person when information is in short supply. "They didn't say who they was or where they was from. But they're lookin' for Jennifer." She stopped to let that settle in before going on. "They're definitely strangers t' Clevis. Didn't know nuthin' about the town. I ast 'em if they come in from Jensen or from Plum, and they didn't know for sure—hadn't really been payin' attention, but it was a mountain road, they said. So I told 'em they'd gone right past her street, that she lived right at the end of Hazel Lane—couldn't miss it. They looked at each other, sort of worried, then ast about where they might get a bit o' lunch. I told 'em Matt 'ud still be servin' lunch, even though it is closer t' two o'clock than one. Is Jennifer expectin' company?"

Randy raised his eyebrows and shook his head. "Not that I know of. Ellen might know."

"When she came in earlier t' get her mail, she said she was makin' lasagna for Nola Mae's birthday tomorrow, but she didn't say nothin' about other folks comin'. I hope it's all right, my sendin' 'em to her. She's had trouble enough this year without any more landin' on her doorstep. Maybe you could check to make sure everything's okay."

"Sure thing. We'll give her a call later to find out what's going on. Glad you're looking out for her, Frieda."

"You say the car's still out front? So 'tis," she said, peering through the murky window. "I guess they did go across the street to eat. Couldn't be too close friends or they'd a had lunch with her. Who in the world could they be?"

"Even now," mused Nathan, "it's hard to figure out why God went to such lengths in His siege of the fortress. It nearly cost your life, and it did cost Rosalie's."

Jennifer looked up in alarm. "Now wait a minute! You're not thinking God took Rosalie just for its effect on you!"

"No . . . but I can't say it didn't cross my mind," he smiled. "No, I listened to you that day up here after her funeral, and I heard what you were saying. Your Hound of Heaven went to work on me, breathing down my neck, and I was undone."

She sat up. "*My* Hound of Heaven? How do you know about that?"

"It was open on your desk when you were sick, lying in wait. I couldn't even blame it on you because you didn't know I was coming. I read it—and read it—and read it. It all fit—the loves, nature, pulling my life down on my own head, and even the bit about children. After you talked to me, I had this inescapable conviction that God was the only one who could possibly love me and that He had been trying all these years to get me to stop running."

"But," she frowned, "I didn't say a word about that. You wouldn't let me. The Lord knows I wanted to, but you cut me off before—"

"I know. But I was already being shouted at, and I didn't need—didn't want, maybe?—to hear the same thing from you. It was more than I could deal with right then. I realized afterward that I knocked you about pretty badly that day in more ways than one, but it was at that point that things began to turn around, and I was sorry for what I had said and done."

Tears came to her eyes. "I felt so bad for you—"

"I know you did. And your words did have an effect, but not quite the way you expected."

She nodded slowly. "Ellen was saying just the other day that none of us really knows what we're doing. The things we try hardest at and expect the most of often don't seem to amount to much, but some little insignificant thing turns out to have had a tremendous impact on somebody—like Nola Mae's book being open on the desk. I guess God likes to work that way, using fools and failure just so we don't get mixed up about who's really doing the job."

His smile held a trace of sadness. "Fools and failure—the entrance requirements to the club! That's what it says in the book. I got hold of a Bible and read it through and—"

"*The whole thing?*"

"Yes. Why?"

"Good grief! I'm just surprised, that's all. How long did it take you?"

"Oh, a week or so. It seemed to tie together. I didn't think it would way back in the Old Testament, but I changed my mind further along. Anyway, it was the same God of mercy and forgiveness all the way through, and for

191

the first time there was a glimmer of hope in the long mountain night."

He sat absently examining her fingers, then began to laugh. "Magnificent! The Hound of Heaven brings The Fox to bay! What do you think of that?"

"And tames it!" Jennifer squeezed his hand delightedly as she thought of *The Little Prince*.

"But a lot hinged on you after that. That afternoon you laid for me near the river—if you'd even looked at me cross-eyed, I would've been off and running again. But you didn't, and you even wanted to be with me. I wasn't sure what you had in mind, but I decided to take you at face value and see what happened. What happened was that Tikki didn't make it up the mountain; Justin and Nathan were the only ones left to beat the tar out of the boys and bury Orley."

"You could've fooled me when I heard the ruckus with the boys! Was Justin as good as Tikki at turning the air blue?"

A sheepish grin on his face, he rubbed a scuff mark from his shoe. "Well, Justin was allus one fer doin' a job right, an' he done a mighty fine piece o' work that day, y' got t' admit. Furthermore, a man doesn't knock out a third of his vocabulary overnight, y' know. You try it sometime!"

"Where did you learn to build coffins?"

"Humph—by doing it! Three times."

"You built Sara's, too?"

"Yes. Grandfather was a cabinetmaker by trade, and he taught me what little I know, but especially to do a job with care and pride. I didn't have much pride to invest, but I sure poured in an awful lot of care."

"They were beautiful. Orley's was the last thing I looked at from your hand, and it spoke of you as well as about Orley."

An expression of tenderness that was almost pain came

over his face. "I think the hardest thing I ever did in my whole life—aside from burning my shirt, of course—was walking away from you at the river. I knew Tikki had to die for both of us to be free, and I knew what I was risking by turning you back over to Corey, but it had to be. There was no other way. I could only hope your love was strong enough to come through the fire."

Her fingers sifted through the pine needles. "You don't know it, but you spoke to me in those awful days, too—through a song Nola Mae plays a lot, about a lover who goes away. In one of the verses he says,

> Dear one, well dost thou know
> Why fond lovers must part:
> Wherefore falters thy faith?
> Why so timid thy heart?

"I could hear you saying that to me, and it helped."

"I know that song! What's the name of it—something about water, flowing water or something—"

"'Waters Ripple and Flow'—"

"That's it. 'Waters ripple and flow, slowly passes each—'"

"Oh, come on! You don't know that, too!"

He threw back his head and laughed. "We sang it in high school, in one of the choruses I was stuffed into."

He paused as an earlier thought returned. "Jennifer, I'm pretty sure I know how you feel about Corey. Are you positive, though," his eyes twinkling, "you want to give up that fine mother-in-law? But," the laughter died, "I don't know that the one I have to offer would be much better, or even if—" He broke off and then brightened again after a moment. "Well, that's neither here nor there. I promise that you won't have in-law problems, even if it means moving to Australia to get away from them!"

He pulled her to her feet. "So—it looks as though the

choice boils down to the son of Jupiter and Juno, or the son of Orpheus and St. Cecelia—take your pick . . . what's the matter?" He looked closely at her troubled face. "Do those choices distress you?"

"Oh, Nathan, I love you with all my heart and soul, as I never could love Corey. But I'm not beautiful or talented like Lynn, and I don't want you to find that I'm not what she was and be unhap—"

He stopped her with a kiss. "Shh! Enough! You're not Lynn. She's dead, and it's been dealt with once and for all. Even if she were alive, I'm not sure I could be happy—now—with her. You are *Jennifer*, a special, unique woman I know and love. I won't ask you to marry me right away because you need to get better acquainted with Nathan. And there are still a good many mountains out there that we have to work our way over. One of these is—" his face became grave, "is talking with Lynn's folks and whatever may issue from that."

Jennifer's eyes widened. "Oh—you mean—would they turn you over to the police?"

"I don't know—it's possible, though they're not the vindictive sort, and it has been a long time. But there's a pretty good chance of my having some time to catch up on my reading." He squeezed her shoulder. "Does that scare you off?"

"No. But is it all right if I hope and pray that it'll all work out so there won't be anything like that?"

"Go ahead. But we need to face it and count the cost. The possibility is there. Are you able to live with that—"

"—for my sake?" They said the words together and laughed.

"Nathan, I've lived with a whole lot worse for your sake. It may be a mountain, but it's not the biggest one. The view from here is all downhill!"

"And the mountain that really matters has already turned!"

They had moved to the edge of the knoll, and as they gazed down the river valley to the hills rolling off into the distance, Jennifer recited the words, their impact full and shining in her eyes:

> Lo, the mountain has turn'd,
>   Now the vict'ry is thine;
> Now my happiness dawns,
>   Now shall freedom be mine!

Slowly they began to descend the slope, each wrapped in supreme happiness until the double thump of car doors brought their heads up.

"Who in the world is that?" Jennifer strained to make out the moving figures near the house. "It's too early for Nola Mae to be back—no, it's not her car. It's a woman I don't recognize. You don't suppose Hilda is here with reinforcements? No, there's a man—he's going up to the door."

They stopped, and Jennifer suddenly became aware of an enormous tension in Nathan. She glanced up and saw a cold hardness on his face.

"Nathan—what is it? Do you know them? Who are they?" But she might as well have been talking to a tombstone. His eyes were steel, his body a tightly coiled spring. She sensed the strange negative alchemy that was seeking to destroy their hard-won victory. Within him, the wisdom of twelve years' sheer survival was rushing to throw up a new fortress around his terribly exposed self. He stared down the hill, his mouth a thin line, scarcely breathing, heedless of Jennifer's frightened questions.

She was afraid—for him, for herself. It was as though she had had the Tikki she loved for two brief hours and was now watching him turn back to the Tikki she feared. She had to do or say something quickly, but there was no time. The two below had spotted them and were moving in their direction.

Jennifer, heart pounding, spoke with all the command she could muster. "Nathan—look at me!" She tugged at his arm. *"Look at me!"* She reached up and turned his head to face her. His eyes softened ever so slightly and held hers, even as they heard voices calling from below.

She took hold of both his hands. "Nathan, you are *free*. You are free from sin, free from guilt, free from the past, free from hatred. *You are free to love.* Nathan, do you love me? Tell me, Nathan, *do you love me now*?"

For what seemed like forever, he gazed into her eyes. Then his tension began seeping away and his breathing became normal. Color returned to his face and he closed his eyes, the same cloak of infinite sadness over him that she had observed when she was ill.

When he opened his eyes once again, a crooked, almost self-mocking smile came to his lips. "Yes, dearest Jennifer, I do love you." He put his arm around her and drew her once again down the hill. "And now you'd better come meet my parents."

LITERARY DATA

Books

The First Circle, Aleksandr Solzhenitsyn, pp. 33, 313, 575 quoted on pp. 79–80.

East and West, Aleksandr Solzhenitsyn, p. 6 quoted on p. 172.

The Little Prince, Antoine de Saint-Exupéry, pp. 110, 192.

Poetry

William Blake, "Little Lamb" p. 59.

John Keats, from "Ode On a Grecian Urn" p. 172.

Christina Rossetti, "As Ointment Poured Forth" pp. 48, 60.

Francis Thompson, from *Ecclesiastical Ballads*
  "Lilium Regis" p. 81.
  "The Veteran of Heaven" p. 80.
  "The Hound of Heaven" pp. 81–82.

Music

Appalachian Spring, Aaron Copland, pp. 9, 90.

Sixth Symphony, "Pathetique," Peter Ilyitch Tchaikovsky, p. 91.

"Waters Ripple and Flow," Czecho-Slovak folk song, arranged by Deems Taylor. The text is printed in full on pp. 160–161 and in part throughout.

Requiem, Johannes Brahms, pp. 124–125.

Festival Te Deum, Benjamin Britten, p. 110.